CIM

Principles of Computer- integrated Manufacturing

D0188481

CIM

Principles of Computer-integrated Manufacturing

Jean-Baptiste Waldner
Ecole Supérieure d'Electricité
Ecole Nationale d'Ingénieurs de Belfort
Institut National des Sciences et Techniques Nucléaires France

Translated by
W. J. Duffin, UK

JOHN WILEY & SONS
Chichester • New York • Brisbane • Toronto • Singapore

First published as *CIM: Les nouvelles perspectives de la production* © 1990 Bordas Paris

Copyright © 1992 by John Wiley & Sons Ltd,
                Baffins Lane, Chichester,
                West Sussex PO19 1UD, England

Other Wiley Editorial Offices

John Wiley & Sons, Inc., 605 Third Avenue, New York, NY 10158-0012, USA

Jacaranda Wiley Ltd, G.P.O. Box 859, Brisbane, Queensland 4001, Australia

John Wiley & Sons (Canada) Ltd, 22 Worcester Road, Rexdale, Ontario M9W 1L1, Canada

John Wiley & Sons (SEA) Pte Ltd, 37 Jalan Pemimpin #05-04, Block B, Union Industrial Building, Singapore 2057

Library of Congress Cataloging-in-Publication Data

Waldner, Jean-Baptiste.
    [CIM, les nouvelles perspectives de la production.   English]
    Principles of computer integrated manufacturing / Jean-Baptiste Walder : translated by W.J. Duffin.
       p.   cm.
    Translation of: CIM, les nouvelles perspectives de la production.
    Includes bibliographical references and index.
    ISBN 0 471 93450 X
    1. Computer integrated manufacturing systems.   I. Title.
  TS155.6.W3513   1992
  670'.285—dc20   92-9522
                                                        CIP

British Library Cataloguing in Publication Data

A catalogue record for this book is available from the British Library

ISBN 0 471 93450 X

Typeset in 10/12½pt Palatino by Acorn Bookwork, Salisbury, Wilts
Printed and bound in Great Britain by Biddles Ltd, Guildford and King's Lynn

Contents

Foreword

Over the last 40 years, we have moved steadily from an economy marked by an abundance of demand to a market dominated by supply. During what are sometimes called the '30 glorious years' (1945–75), the manufacturing world organized itself to respond to growth with large-scale production of a single product or similar products. Today, it has to satisfy a demand that has become increasingly complex and diverse: small-scale production of many models with frequent and rapid changes. A business wishing to remain in good health must respond at once to unpredictable and abrupt variations in the market. In such a context, *reliability* and *flexibility* become the keywords in the production process.

In a family business, most of the functions are fulfilled by the head of the company alone, who then has to be responsible for purchasing, production, personnel, sales, finance and so on. The larger the business becomes, the more these functions are distributed between a number of units with different responsibilities (vertical divisions). The danger then arises that each of the specialized units will pursue its own objectives without paying any attention to the prior need to seek the optimum overall objective, i.e. satisfying the customer at the lowest cost. An excessive compartmentalization of the functions can only lead to sluggishness and long delays in reacting to market changes: a fatal risk in the present climate.

It is at this point that the author of the present book comes to the rescue of company heads. He demythologizes the most recent jargon and fashionable concepts in management, which everybody uses without always having a precise knowledge of their meaning: CIM, Kanban systems, SMED, 'tight flow', just-in-time systems, etc. He fits all these isolated concepts into an ordered package and, in a futuristic vision, puts forward a new approach to production. Herein lies the great merit of this book, since only a few publications dealing with CIM in an integrated fashion have appeared so far.

Computer-integrated manufacturing or CIM has become the key concept in future company strategy. Because it is sometimes referred to as an integrated system of production, the field of CIM has appeared to be restricted literally to factory production alone. In fact, the objective of CIM is much more extensive: it aims to help with all business functions, not only with production, and to establish close, systematic and frequent relationships between the various functional units by the optimum use of one of the basic resources of business: *information*.

When it is adopted CIM involves a profound transformation in the structure of firms. Until that point is reached, information systems are usually designed and set up in 'islands'. The first information systems for management and control were developed 25 years ago at the same time as numerical control systems for programming the operations carried out by machine tools, while computer-aided design (CAD) has already been in use in R & D offices for some 15 years.

The problem now is one of integrating the functions into a whole. The information systems installed in each functional unit must carry out their specific tasks, but must also use the information generated by other units and send the necessary data both upstream and downstream. An integrated information system means a more intensive use of data-processing facilities and the development of a consistent and evolving computerized structure incorporating the four standard elements: computers, databases, user applications and communication systems using local area networks (LANs).

The potential benefits are very great. An investigation carried out in 1986 in several large US companies showed that, after setting up a first level of integration, one could expect an increase in productivity of about 120%, an improvement in quality of about 140% and an increase in the use of equipment of between 50 and 300%.

These figures may seem surprising, but they are due mainly to (1) investment in new techniques or improvements in techniques already being used (SMED, etc.,) and (2) an accurate, rapid and efficient information system.

Because of the high stakes involved it is the responsibility of general management to lay down the directions to be taken. This implies that all the main participants must be involved in the changes, and it should not be a question of making it the concern only of technical staff. When the CIM spirit is acquired, the boundaries between functional units become blurred. Decision-makers at all levels then examine their projects from two viewpoints: their profitability to the ordering department and their contribution to the whole company.

A modern and competitive company is characterized by a willingness to remove boundaries and by the development of cooperation between all the functional units. Productivity is no longer the result of a technique but is the result of a system in which human beings are the cornerstones. Finally, and this is very comforting, well-conducted automation relies on human beings who are and who remain the principal participants in change and the driving forces behind it.

The new approach to production represented by CIM could be very simply entitled 'produce differently'. It implies an upheaval in current organization, breaking down F. W. Taylor's system of parcelling out tasks, and enriching the content of work through a greater exercise of skills by making individuals responsible at all levels and involving them fully in the collective effort.

Technology is evolving and changing ever more rapidly, products have ever-shorter useful lives, the supply of goods is becoming more broadly based and diversified, customers are becoming increasingly fickle. There is, however, no need for industry to be fatalistic in the face of modernization. The resources in human intelligence, the possibilities of individual development and the still unexplored initiative present in every one of us, are inexhaustible. Even so, it is essential that those at the top should motivate the whole workforce sufficiently to provide a company with the capacity to adapt.

The author has amply demonstrated this: CIM is both a wonderful vehicle for future progress and a genuine attitude of mind.

G. Perrier
Director of the Peugeot Production Centre, Sochaux
Chairman of the Société Industrielle de Mulhouse

List of Commonly used Abbreviations

(see also Appendix 2)

CAD	Computer-aided design
CADD	Computer-aided drawing and drafting
CAE	Computer-aided engineering
CAM	Computer-aided manufacturing
CASE	Computer-aided software engineering
CIM	Computer-integrated manufacturing
CNC	Computer numerically controlled
DBMS	Database management system
FEM	Finite element method
FMS	Flexible manufacturing system
ILAN	Industrial LAN
JIT	Just-in-time
KBS	Knowledge-based system
LAN	Local area network
MIS	Management information system
MPS	Master (production) schedule
MRP	Material requirements planning
MRP2	Manufacturing resource planning
NC	Numerically controlled
OSI	Open systems interconnection
PIC	Production and inventory control
PLC	Programmable logic controller
TQC	Total quality control

Translator's Note

Several modifications have been made to the French text for this edition. The author has added new sections on knowledge-based systems to Chapter 6 and has provided some relevant case studies as Appendices 3 and 4. Where appropriate, and with the author's approval, several slight changes have been made to the original text in order to adapt it for English-speaking readers.

I am very grateful to Dr Mike Dooner of the Department of Engineering Design and Manufacture at the University of Hull for reading the whole manuscript, for considerable help with English terminology in the field and for suggestions which have enhanced the clarity of the translation.

1 Integrated Production and the CIM Method

1.1 INTRODUCTION

Throughout human history, and especially in the history of science and technology, new ideas have never been universally accepted—there has usually been some division of opinion. A natural inclination to be fashionable, which is a common response to any innovation, is always opposed by a tendency to be conservative or, more often, by a traditional attitude which argues against the change.

The high technology used to improve productivity in the manufacturing sector has by no means escaped this fate. If the sheer volume of published articles and books discussing it is anything to go by, it must be a long time since any technico-economic controversy has caused so much ink to flow.

Yet, although the complete automation of manufacturing processes was the futuristic dream of most industrialists at the end of the 1960s, the present-day consensus over the 'Factory of the Future' does not seem to be as strong as it was. Such a change in attitude can hardly be the result of technology not living up to its promise: it is, rather, due to a fundamental change in the rules of the market during the 1970s. Objectives concerned with nothing but productivity gave way to others more concerned with flexibility and quality. The demands of competition between companies created a veritable explosion in their trading inventories.

As a result of this new climate, a different mode of industrial organization was developed in Japan, a mode which aimed at increasing the responsiveness and thus the flexibility of a company by reducing the administrative procedures involved in management and control. These ideas, which are based on giving responsibility to personnel engaged directly in production activities, also revealed that over-automation of processes could have undesirable consequences. For example, it very often turned out that the functions performed by very complex systems based on electronic and computer technology could equally well be carried out by elementary manual procedures or by simple mechanical devices. In short, the notion of simplicity had been lost. Computerization had become a universal and automatic response in every sector of a company, and no attempt was made to find a less complex alternative to a proposed procedure. In the social sphere, too, the new approach seemed to bring a worthwhile response in a reevaluation of their jobs by the workers and in an enrichment of the tasks they performed, the lack of which is so often blamed on an organizational structure based on the principles of F. W. Taylor.

Reports of some of the shortcomings of over-automation were not long in shattering the predictions of those who called for the total integration of production by computerization. The setback was immediately exploited by the opponents of complete automation, some of whom even saw in this a new 'back to basics' movement, which they were quick to use to their advantage. However, to rely only on human effort and on a careful redistribution of responsibility in a company, and to rule out the eventual unification of the exchange of information through a computerized system, seemed quite as unreasonable as the unconditional automation that was being so strongly contested.

The most efficient Japanese companies that originated the new organizational principles continue to put their faith in automation. The labour costs of standard assembly lines have fallen from 25% to 10%, and even to 5% of the total cost of the product. Some highly automated plants, such as that of the car manufacturer Toyota, say that they can operate at 70% capacity without losing money. The numerical control manufacturer Fujitsu Fanuc even reaches its profitability threshold at a utilization of 10% of its capacity. This flexibility could only be attained by a reduction in the work force as the result of an expansion in automated activities.

From the macroeconomic viewpoint, while highly automated companies get through a recession by remaining clearly profitable even at a modest level of use, the evolution from a highly labour-intensive industry to a highly equipment-intensive industry is contributing to the fight against inflation inasmuch as the relative proportion of labour costs in total manufacturing costs can only increase when wages rise or when sales fall.

The intention of this book is not to add emotional opinions to the debate on 'computerized control of everything', but rather to attempt to describe all the techniques available for the integration of production, the principles of such techniques and the ways in which they are designed and implemented.

1.2   COMPUTER-INTEGRATED MANUFACTURING: STAKING ALL ON TECHNOLOGY

An integrated system of production does not necessarily imply that computerized systems have to be used. The expression 'to integrate' should mainly be understood as 'to remove the boundaries between' the functions of a company which, for justifiable historical reasons, were previously split up (see Sec. 1.3).

For most of the time during which a machine, a workshop or factory is being set up, those in charge are mainly concerned with the machines and the equipment. It is only later, and to a lesser extent, that they become concerned about logistical problems in the flow of materials and parts.

There are many ways, using little or no technology, of enabling a company to move towards integrated production: improved configuration of workstations, regrouping of workshops and factories, rationalization of products and working methods, etc. However, the development of large computer memories and powerful microprocessors has rapidly lowered the cost of computing facilities. In less than 20 years the power of RAM chips has increased from 1 kbit (1970) to 4 Mbits (1989), a factor of 4000.

The use of digital techniques in industrial equipment has become increasingly intensive, to the point where almost all business sectors now exploit the properties of firmware-based systems, ranging from the automatically regulated control station of a heat-treatment furnace, through applications on the host computer to the operation of numerically controlled machine tools.

At the beginning of the 1980s, attempts to integrate the various functions of industrial firms by making use of the common data-storage and data-processing characteristics of the individual items of hardware faced the problem of communication between incompatible systems. The unification of all the computer systems through a common network was so important to firms that it led to the development of norms and standards for intercommunication (ISO, MAP, TOP, etc.—see Sec. 2.6).

Alongside this, the concept of computer integrated manufacturing (CIM) was born. This involves both the automation of physical operations (through computer-aided design (CAD), flexible manufacturing systems, automatic storage and handling, etc.) and a conceptual methodology combining all these components within an overall management information system.

If the integration of production is assumed to be an essential aim for the majority of manufacturing firms, CIM is one method by which it may be achieved. The investment and the effort required for adaptation may not make it the easiest of methods to implement, but in the long term it is probably the only one that can guarantee the complete integration of all the functions.

1.3   FROM COTTAGE INDUSTRIES TO THE INTEGRATED PLANT

1.3.1   The cultural heritage

When we look at industrial organization today, we can see that the scars of the Taylor system are still evident. The change from a quantity-based to a quality-based culture in our manufacturing production systems has called into question a model that provided a world-wide standard for industry for many decades.

The development of large companies from the end of the last century led in the most natural possible way to the principles of the division of labour and the specialization of tasks:

(1) Most of today's large industrial firms were founded by one or two men (e.g. Ford, Hewlett-Packard, Bull, Boeing, Dassault, Renault, Citroën, Rolls-Royce).

(2) The founders knew the company intimately and knew at any moment what was happening.

(3) Expansion of the companies made it impossible to centralize all the information and the management of all the tasks through a single person: the tasks were split up and allocated to specific groups with special skills.

(4) At the same time the tasks were carried out more efficiently because of the specialization, thus increasing productivity.

(5) More complex ways of transporting materials and parts and of exchanging information were created, and this led to a considerable increase in general costs.

(6) Greater management and control of the resultant complex system was necessary (see Sec. 1.3.3).

The adverse effects were for a long time concealed by the push system in force at the beginning of this century.

Organizations based on the Taylor system were apparently justified even more when US industry had to provide the equipment needed by the armed forces during the Second World War. The logic of the division of labour enabled those not serving in the forces to be trained quickly in production tasks, and enabled better advantage to be taken of the increasingly scarce skilled workers in controlling and coordinating the performance of the tasks.

Post-war society was characterized by a proliferation of unskilled workers and a corresponding lack of skilled workers. At the same time the appetites of consumers created by the privations of war created a great and frustrated demand. The Taylor system was perfectly adapted to this situation and was of enormous help in bringing the economy out of its period of shortages.

With the end of what may be called the '30 glorious years' (1945–75), we saw the relative strengths of supply and demand being reversed. The economy entered a period of abundance, so that the principles underlying the Taylor system lost their benefits and began to be modified. We would have been better advised to abandon them altogether, and the harmful effects of not doing so were not long in making themselves felt.

In such a system, problems are dealt with systematically one by one according to the precepts of the division of labour, and no consideration is given to the overall production process. In order to set up a dialogue between functions that are studied and optimized in isolation, extremely cumbersome administrative procedures are supported by staff engaged in indirect activities. As a result, it is by no means rare to find companies whose overheads make up more than 20% of the direct manufacturing costs.

1.3.2 Justifying the role of the computer

The advent of processing power to deal with the flow of information, which first produced data-processing systems and then transaction-oriented systems, seemed capable of carrying out the coordination and control procedures which until then had been taken on by ever-increasing numbers of staff engaged in indirect activities.

Instead of tackling the real causes of a problem, the tendency was to minimize its consequences. In addition, the cost of setting up increasingly powerful data-processing systems meant that support could no longer be given to the concept of automating the tasks of coordination.

Many examples, which have contributed to the reputation won by Japanese firms in recent years, show that the solution lies in a process of *simplification* and subsequent *unification* of companies. Such a process can be stated in the following form:

(1) Simplification (eliminating all useless or redundant tasks which contribute no added value to the product).

(2) Integration (recombining or decompartmentalizing the functions of the company).

(3) (Possible) application of the appropriate CIM technology (see Chapter 2).

It is then clear that data-processing facilities, working within a unified system, are no longer being used merely to replace manual tasks, but are contributing to the integration of production and thus providing a real added-value financial return.

1.3.3 A little cybernetics

Although we shall not delve very deeply into technological questions, it needs to be stressed that the theory of dynamic systems does further the understanding of certain problems: in particular, that of managing complexity in industry and that related to the simplification that must be undertaken before any reorganization of a management system. These are matters of primary importance at the present time.

The concept of a 'system' in the mathematical sense applies to any process, whether physical, economic or social. Thus, any company or even its component parts (factory, workshop, etc.) may be considered as a system.

The complexity of a system may be modelled by the *variety* of the various states which it is capable of adopting (Fig. 1.1). When several systems are combined together, their varieties or complexities do not add but multiply (Fig. 1.2).

Controlling a system involves associating it with another system whose role is to keep the variety of the results or objectives as small as possible. For example, if the system to be investigated is a car and its control system

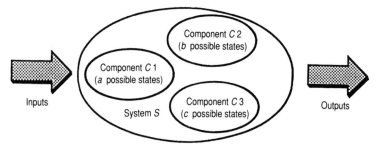

Fig. 1.1.
The variety of a system with several components. S has three components C1, C2, C3 capable of being in a, b and c different states respectively. The variety V of the system is abc, or a^3 if $a = b = c$.

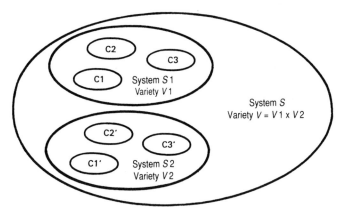

Fig. 1.2.
The variety of a combination of systems.

is the driver, the objective will be to keep the distance between the vehicle and the roadside virtually constant over the whole of the journey.

The variety of the results or objectives (V_0) cannot be less than

$$V_0 = \frac{V}{V_c} = \frac{\text{variety of system to be managed}}{\text{variety of control system}}$$

Since the variety of the results is a minimum, it can only decrease if the variety of the control system increases.

This expresses the *law of requisite variety*, which establishes that only the variety of the control system can reduce that resulting from the process to be controlled, and that only complexity can destroy complexity.

This fundamental principle shows that the regulation of a system in the strict sense demands a control system whose complexity is equal to or greater than that of the system to be managed.

In view of the prohibitive number of dimensions which such a system would then take on, it is easy to appreciate the importance of the procedure for simplifying the functions of the company before any attempt at their integration, even when using facilities as powerful as the largest computers. This step is an essential prerequisite for the success of any CIM project.

1.4   WHAT IS INVOLVED

In cybernetic theories, a company is often compared to a living creature which, to ensure its own survival, must respond to the following challenge: 'How can we be competitive in the market in the face of competition?'

The rate at which technology is renewed, the expanding supply side and the world-wide spread of industrialization have forced managers to widen their horizons and become better informed about all the pressures that affect the strategic and tactical plans of their companies. The ultimate goal of every industrial enterprise must be to achieve the best performance as regards costs, completion times, quality and flexibility in the face of variations in demand.

A large number of investigations show that the present concerns of general managers in the East are mainly the reduction of costs (both indirect and that of materials), a high quality of production and an improvement in responsiveness to demand.

The objective common to the whole of manufacturing industry in the current market is to supply *a good-quality product at the right time*. This imperative will manifest itself technically by the manufacture of completely reliable products in small quantities at the lowest possible cost with very short completion times. The terms *flexibility* and *quality*, now occurring very frequently in the vocabulary of the business community, sum up very well the present strategic aims in matters of production.

1.4.1   CIM: a standardized model of the company

It is essential to have a model available in order to guide a dynamic system, for example to manage a company. The state of the system must therefore be represented as faithfully as possible, which means that the development of the real system must be simulated as rapidly and as accurately as possible.

One of the fundamental alms of CIM is to provide, for all those taking part in an enterprise, an appropriate view of the system in which they are evolving: an overall synthesis for the managers and a specialized and detailed view for the operational staff.

The standardization of such a model is clearly of importance for learning about it, for taking advantage of the information provided by the various outputs from it, for maintenance facilities and for the development of a strategy common to several units in a group. Work now in progress (CAM–I, NBS and ITI in the USA, the CIM–OSA and CNMA projects of the ESPRIT programme in Europe) attest to the increasing importance of standardization in the world of industrial information technology (see CIM and Standardization Appendix 1).

1.4.2   Reduction of costs and manufacturing lead times

Considerable extra costs can be created by developing production units as the need arises, and with no strategic plan. Machines and equipment are installed where there is room for them; new products are made by using the existing resources to the full; parts and materials are mixed at random: all this has the sole aim of exploiting the available means of production to the maximum.

Considered in isolation, all the investments made by a firm are generally justified. However, it too often happens that they create complications and disorder at the overall organizational level (chaotic flow of materials, hunting around for parts, cumbersome administrative procedures, waiting, proliferation of hierarchical levels) which will increase indirect costs and hinder the responsiveness of the production process.

Costs of materials and indirect costs often account for more than 90% of the total cost. A reduction in these undoubtedly means a better integration of production, which will come about through reducing the number of hierarchical levels, through an easing of the administrative procedures and a complete intermeshing of the various functions in the firm (supply with production, marketing with planning, etc.). The efficiency of communication in external relations with customers and suppliers can also be improved by replacing our traditional contractual rules (bargaining and uncertainty in relationships) with a solid adherence to common aims (see Sec. 2.6).

On the other hand, since the use of advanced production technology will enable direct labour costs to be reduced from about 30% to 10% of the total cost, it is then no longer necessarily appropriate to invest too high a level of resources in them.

Extremely fatalistic assumptions have often led to an acceptance of a high cost of waiting, representing at least a fifth of the cost of direct labour, if not a quarter. The shortening or even the elimination of such sterile waiting times is the basic aim of 'just-in-time' (JIT) production systems (see Chapter 4). It should be noted that, in the mechanical engineering industry, pieceparts spend only 5% of their time on the machines, about 30% of this time being devoted to machining proper.

1.4.3   Total quality control

Before the second oil crisis, the quality-control function was isolated from the production process and this is still the case today in many Western firms. It was accepted that up to 10%, and sometimes more, of the potential production was rejected. Since the workers were not in any way worried by such a level, they concerned themselves merely with the volume produced and this very often only contributed to a worsening of the effect.

After 1973, industrialists learnt a fundamental lesson from the oil crisis: no resource is inexhaustible, so that any form of wastage must be avoided. The principle implicit in this lesson can be applied by integrating quality control into the production process, giving rise to the concept of total quality control (TQC). This is based on five objectives:

(1) To aim at zero defects (and no longer at an acceptable quality level).

(2) To make everybody in the organization responsible for quality.

(3) To prevent defects occurring (preventive maintenance and automation techniques).

(4) To implement simple criteria for measuring quality.

(5) To measure quality automatically at suitable points.

TQC relies technically on a system in which the control data acquired in real time are used to correct the production process dynamically by means of a closed-loop feedback system (Fig. 1.3). This method demands a unified and transaction-based information system using databases and the unification of all the shared user applications through local area networks (LANs) (see Sec. 2.6).

The concept of self-correction by feedback in real time can be extended to the complete chain from *supplier* through the *producer* to the *customer*. This principle is beginning to take shape in France through value-added networks such as GALIA, ODETTE, etc. These not only provide for

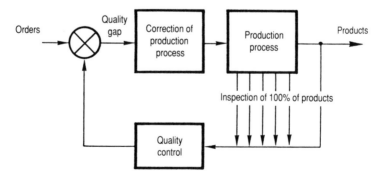

Fig. 1.3.
Quality control using a feedback loop.

exchange of data with suppliers and customers but also offer a set of services and standard procedures activated automatically by processing taking place in the production unit information system. For example, the calculation of material requirements by the production control system generates supply orders and this directly activates orders in the supplier's system. Such a system also enables the product to be completely tracked right from the manufacture of components through to the suppliers' premises.

In the USA this new idea of the supplier as partner, in contrast with the supplier as slave, has given rise to the concept of the *extended firm*. The expression describes the large industrial conglomerates which represent the intermeshed networks of the firms themselves together with their suppliers and subcontractors.

1.5 A CONTINUALLY GROWING MARKET

In 1984, two out of three industrialists thought that CIM was appropriate for their company and 95% of them reckoned that the activities of the firm could be better integrated by using computers.

The investment in computer-based production control in the 1970s formed only a marginal proportion of the overall information technology market. However, the size of the sector has shown unending growth since then and in 1988 represented $68 billion worldwide.

A breakdown of these figures (source BIPE, 1988) shows that the share of the world market taken up by computer-based production and inventory control (PIC), and thus by the 'upper' levels of the management information system (MIS) as defined in Sec. 2.6, amounted to $8.3 billion. This compares with $7.7 billion invested in the ancillary devices, the programmable logic controllers, the local area networks and the controllers that form the 'lower' levels.

Production control is clearly one of the main concerns of industrialists: 95% of them wish to possess a computer-based PIC facility by the beginning of the next decade (source MORI, 1984).

The complete integration of data-processing systems into the production process, and more generally the CIM concept, like all avant-garde technology, suffers from a lack of credibility because of its youth as well as from a natural resistance to change.

However, the major brake on the integration of all the functions of the firm through computerization has long been the poor performance and the lack of standards in the sphere of industrial local area networks (ILANs). This technology (Sec. 2.6), the true unifier of the CIM concept, is currently

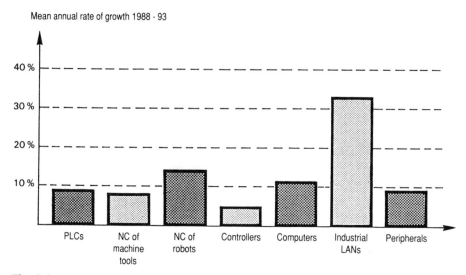

Mean annual rate of growth 1988 - 93

Fig. 1.4.
Growth in the information technology market. (*Source* BIPE—Bureau d'Information et de Prévisions Economiques, 122 Av. Charles de Gaulle, 92522 Neuilly-sur-Seine, France.)

on the way to becoming the leading sector in computerized production if the current growth and future prospects of the market are to be believed (Fig. 1.4).

Moreover, the development of the market has modified the aims of industrial automation methods. Ten years ago, the profitability of computerized production applications was sought exclusively through the improvement of direct productivity (shorter manufacturing lead times) together with the reduction of immobile material (optimization of stocks and of parts in process of manufacture). Today, the quality and variety of what is supplied have become the dominant factors, so that five industrialists out of six invest in computerized production technology with the basic aim of improving the quality of their products.

2 The Technology Available for a CIM Approach

2.1 FROM ISOLATED DATA-PROCESSING SYSTEMS TO A CIM MODEL

Data-processing systems began to permeate the industrial world in the 1960s, first as computing tools for assisting in design and for conventional company management and later, on a more massive scale, as generalized computer-aided systems (PIC, CAD, CAM, etc.).

The different applications were, however, developed independently and, although they can certainly improve the efficiency of the individual section using them, they are far from bringing the benefits of integrated production. The various functions of the company remain isolated and many tasks are performed in an unnecessarily redundant manner (bills of materials retrieved and used at the design department on the CAD system and then recalled and used again on the PIC system at the methods office and in production). The basic rule governing the specification of any integrated information system can be stated as follows: 'Information is introduced into the system (and updated) solely by those who produce it.'

While the integration process requires an effort at the organizational level in a company, it also introduces new constraints for those who supply the hardware and software and for those who provide services, all of whom are responsible for installing the new systems. The applications should be developed within a very wide-ranging strategy of integration and intercommunication.

It has often been observed in the field of science and technology that the discovery of a link between two branches has been of mutual benefit to each other's development. As a result, there is generally an accelerated advance in both. Examples that most easily come to mind are those of the infinitesimal calculus and celestial mechanics, chromosomes and heredity, fractal geometry and meteorology.

A CIM approach would mean that one is concerned not only with the study of the internal characteristics of the various applications that form an integrally automated production environment, but also (and more especially) with their communication properties, i.e. with their capacity for improving the integration of the functions of the company.

2.2   CONTROL OF THE FIRM: THE MASTER SCHEDULE

A manager should be capable of maximizing the use of all the company's resources in order to carry out the agreed policy and attain the strategic objectives. The information system is therefore designed in such a way that the following two factors apply:

(1) All the key data used for decision-making in the company are available, up to date and directly accessible. This enables help to be given to an executive in immediate decisional choices.

(2) The detailed design of the system guarantees that decisions are taken at the appropriate level. Important decisions are then no longer taken at a subordinate level, a factor which can be very costly for the company.

The control function in a firm depends on two facilities:

(1) The *master schedule*, a model based on the company's 'game plan', providing help in medium- to long-term planning decisions. The plan validated in this way will form a contract between management and the representatives of the various functions (see Sec. 3.3).

(2) The bills of materials and, more generally, the *technical database*, which enables the global information dealt with in the master schedule to be worked out in detail (see Sec. 3.2).

2.3   PRODUCT PLANNING, DESIGN AND MANUFACTURE

The ever shorter life cycles of products and the need of the company to be responsive to the demands of the market for new products make it advisable not to deal separately with the design and manufacturing functions. The toing-and-froing between the design stages and those involving the development of the manufacturing process mean that these two tasks must be closely tied together.

Among the computer-aided systems which have increasingly permeated all sectors of world industry, computer-aided design (CAD) is no longer a strange concept. This technology began around 1970 and aims to increase the productivity of engineers and technical staff in design offices by a considerable factor (often greater than 10). The CAD market more than doubled between 1987 and 1990.

Information systems to reinforce production methods have also arrived in the form of computer-aided manufacturing (CAM), which makes it easier to develop production programmes and enables a computer to be used in direct control of operations on numerically controlled (NC) machine tools.

The importance of integrating CAD and CAM in manufacturing a new product, or in improving existing products, has led many industrialists and suppliers of computer systems to consider such an amalgamation (often known as CAD/CAM) as being CIM, but this is a mistake. CAD and CAM originated from two different worlds that had little or no knowledge of each other: CAD involved graphical representation and modelling, CAM involved the production of programs for NC machines. Their integration quickly imposed the establishment of standards for the exchange of data, such as SET, IGES, STEP, VDA in mechanical engineering and EDIF* in electronic engineering.

In a unified approach to design, implementation and production, CAD and CAM must be combined with a function defining the product structure or the technical database management system. This additional function supplements the CAD/CAM data with information (such as dimensional characteristics, costs, replacement components, physical properties and technico-economic features) enabling it to be used more widely in the context of production control.

2.3.1 Computer-aided design

Computer-aided design (CAD) is not a very precise term. In mechanical engineering, a boundary is generally placed between the simple representation of objects (sometimes known as computer-aided drawing and drafting or CADD), and the simulation of the way in which such objects

---

*EDIF = Electronic Design and Interchange Format. For the other abbreviations, see CIM and Standardization, Appendix 1.

function (enabling design in the true sense of the word to be carried out and thus lying within the province of CAD).

In CAD, the operator develops very detailed plans in real time in an interactive mode. At the systems level, the data acquired will form a unique model, two-dimensional (2D) for plane graphic objects or three-dimensional (3D) for spatial models. However, depending on what is required, such a model may be represented in several different ways (a single 3D model may equally well give rise to a perspective drawing or to a set of 2D views). It sometimes happens that, for marketing reasons, we speak of '2½D' systems. This has no mathematical validity and is merely a 3D model in which the third dimension has been 'degraded' by a set of simplifying assumptions (very small thickness, axial symmetry, etc).

The model enables rapid modifications to be made and makes it possible to use standard sub-assemblies and parameterization of parts (e.g. in a graphics model of a roller-bearing where the dimensional parameters will permit the representation of the whole product family). The use of an interactive system also makes the editing of plans a routine matter (by on-screen consultation and updating).

We also distinguish between CAD and the calculation of a solution followed by the use or post-processing of the results, which enables the thousands of figures resulting from computation to be properly under-stood. In the latter case, we use the term *computer-aided engineering* (CAE) in order to extend the idea of CAD to that of the numerical calculation and exploitation of the results (Fig. 2.1).

Normally, CAD enables the object to be modelled for the purpose of subjecting it to simulation in CAE (calculation of the structure in mechan-ical engineering, study of the behaviour of an electronic circuit, etc). The

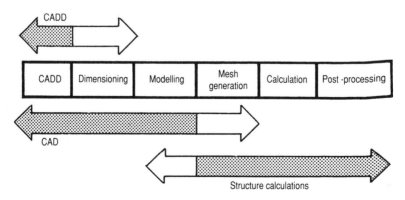

Fig. 2.1.
The areas covered by CAE in mechanical engineering.

aim of CAE is the development of the product in such a way as to optimize industrial production, performance and cost (e.g. by comparison between various possible materials or different designs).

CAE uses information retrieved not only from the CAD system but also from the technical database shared by the computer-based PIC system (Sec. 3.2) in order to analyse the functional characteristics of the part, the product or the process during the design stage, and in order to simulate its performance under varying conditions.

Nowadays there are three basic areas of application included in the generic term CAE (Fig. 2.2):

(1) *Structural analysis and the prediction of reliability and useful life* (modelling by the finite element method or, more generally, applying the laws of physical behaviour to a graphic model provided by CAD).

(2) *The prediction or simulation of performance* (simulations of the responses of dynamic, electronic or logic systems).

(3) *The simulation of an operational process* (modelling of a process or of the operation of a manufacturing plant, systems for the simulation of scheduling, operational research systems).

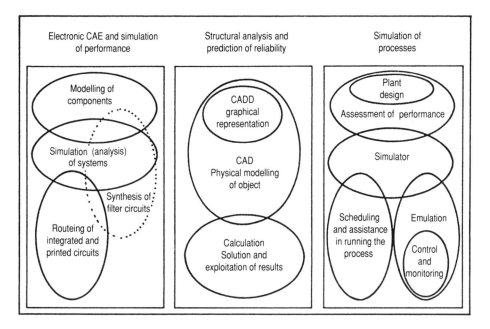

Fig. 2.2.
Computer-aided engineering.

In a present-day CIM context, the integration of (or interface between) a CAD system and the production control application implies that each component or graphic model is indexed in a bill of materials organized at the technical data level and exploited by the production control system (see Sec. 3.2). In this way we attain the maximum efficiency in drawing up estimates and in the preparation of production files (graphic data integrated in real time with the production control system).

2.3.2   The calculation of structures and the finite element method

The finite element method (FEM) is undoubtedly one of the most widely used numerical analysis techniques in the field of mechanical CAD and CAE. The basic idea is to divide the object into a large number of simple elements and apply a physical law to each of them, a task which is relatively easy to perform. The method is used in various areas such as mechanics, heat and electromagnetism, but its commonest application is still in the calculation of mechanical structures.

Structure calculations originated in the nineteenth century with the theory of rods and beams (St Venant, Navier, Castigliano, etc.). With the advent of matrix methods of calculation and the beginnings of data processing as an engineering tool, the same principles gave rise to the FEM.

The first computer programs were produced around 1950 with applications to the calculation of aeronautical structures. During the 1960s, the aerospace, nuclear and shipbuilding industries engaged in further work of the same type (the NASA NASTRAN project). The great names which exist in today's market appeared towards the end of the 1960s: NASTRAN, ANSYS, ASKA, SAP, SYSTUS, etc. The first CAD companies were established in the 1970s with the arrival of graphics terminals and the beginning of interactive systems. Microcomputers and minicomputers, whose power and performance have steadily increased at almost constant prices, finally brought the general use of FEM to the whole of industry after 1985.

No aircraft is now designed without using FEMs. In the automobile industry, too, supercomputers running an FEM program process up to 10 000 nodes for a half car-body, and crash-resistance tests also have been replaced by FEM (French program PAM–CRASH) with many advantages.

By considering an ideal assembly of simple components (which can be considered as small bars or beams), a structure calculation proceeds as follows:

(1) After determining the form of the displacement field in each of the elements, the force–displacement relations are established at the nodes

(points at which elementary components meet each other), i.e. the *local stiffness matrix* of each component.

(2) By a change of the reference coordinate system, these matrices are transferred to a common coordinate system. These are then assembled into a *global stiffness matrix*.

(3) The solution of the system (inversion of the global stiffness matrix) gives the displacements at the nodes. This stage of the process is generally the most laborious part of the calculation.

(4) The loads and stresses are then calculated in each element according to the force–displacement and stress–force relationships.

The FEM extends this type of calculation to continuous media by dividing the domain into as large as possible a number of subdomains with simple shapes (e.g. triangles, rectangles). While the discretization process is obvious for a system consisting of bars, a network of fictitious boundaries and nodes with no physical significance are created in FEM. This network is called the *finite element mesh* of the object.

Instead of directly integrating the local equations of continuity and elasticity over the whole domain determined by the shape of the object, it is possible to proceed from one cell to another, assuming that the computational step is small enough to use a restricted expansion, perfectly adapted to numerical calculation. With an additional assumption about the variation of the field in each element, a particularly simple form for the calculation is obtained: the polynomial form.

An FEM study normally consists of three stages:

(1) retrieving the data and putting them into an appropriate form (geometrical modelling and mesh generation);

(2) calculation;

(3) exploitation of results (post-processing).

The graphical model emerging from CAD is appreciably different from the model required for calculation by FEM. The mere representation of shapes and geometrical characteristics is not enough to model the properties of the structure: It is also necessary to generate a mesh in its interior. Moreover, apart from the difficulties in triangulating a three-dimensional domain, the finite elements must be correctly connected, i.e. there must be continuity of the calculated values at the interface between two adjacent elements.

The temptation to use the graphics CAD model directly very often leads to failure. Cases of an automatic translation from such a model to finite elements are exceptionally rare. The natural way used at present is to pass through an underlying geometrical model (support surfaces, envelopes, etc.) which are then divided up into simple elements.

The mesh generation techniques now available can be classified according to the type of algorithm used for the discretization. They fall into one of three groups:

(1) *Incremental mesh generation,* an almost manual technique first developed around 1975, in which the user defines the first element. The user then indicates a direction and an increment in a given reference frame, together with the number of repetitions to be carried out. The 'row' of elements obtained in this way is duplicated in another direction and the method is repeated until the whole domain is covered by the mesh (Fig. 2.3). This type of mesh generation means that the user has to be fully conversant with all the numberings in the model. This means that specialist engineers are required to implement the method and each model carries the 'imprint' of its originator.

(2) *Propagated mesh generation* in which the user first divides the domain into macro-elements incorporating opposite sides, and then propagates in each of these macro-elements a number of subdivisions imposed by the user over opposite boundaries (Fig. 2.4). One difficulty with this lies in making the nodes on the common boundaries coincide.

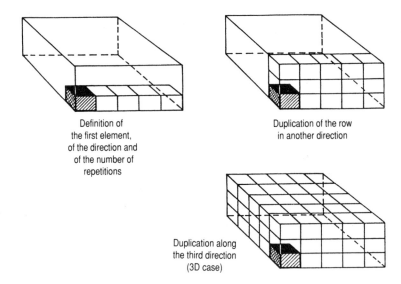

Definition of
the first element,
of the direction and
of the number of
repetitions

Duplication of the row
in another direction

Duplication along
the third direction
(3D case)

Fig. 2.3.
Incremental mesh generation.

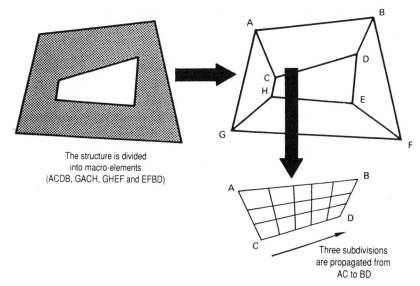

The structure is divided
into macro-elements
(ACDB, GACH, GHEF and EFBD)

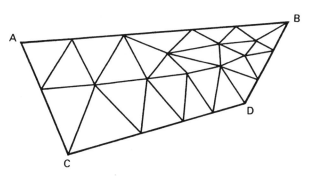

Three subdivisions
are propagated from
AC to BD

Fig. 2.4.
Propagated mesh generation.

Methods (1) and (2) were first-generation automatic mesh generators.

(3) *Mesh generation at the boundaries* or *free mesh generation* (Fig. 2.5), first marketed in 1984, is still not perfect for 3D work. It is a form of automatic mesh generation which produces distinctly more elements than an expert would have produced in the incremental method. This leads to solution times that are often 100 times longer and hence require a very powerful processor.

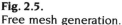

Fig. 2.5.
Free mesh generation.

2.3.3   The simulation of electronic and automatic systems

When an electronic system (or a dynamic system in the broad sense) is not too large, it is always possible to study it experimentally even if the investigation should prove to be a long one. The use of computer programs, on the other hand, may enable such results to be obtained by avoiding any experimentation at the design stage: the behaviour of the system is simulated, i.e. experiments on a mock-up are replaced by numerical analysis on a computer.

This involves the schematic representation of the system or of its elements by models as close as possible to reality. It is then necessary to set up the equations of the system, followed by their solution using analytical or numerical methods. Finally, the results must be supplied to the user in the most practical form (diagrams, graphs, etc.).

Computer simulation has many advantages: it enables rapid changes to be made in the circuit through the conversational mode of present-day applications; it facilitates parametric and statistical studies of the circuit and studies of parasitic phenomena; it also allows the different elements to be 'decorrelated', an impossible approach in an experimental study.

Most of the present analogue simulation programs are analytical (the user program is supplied with the description of the model whose behaviour is to be studied and the simulator returns the results just as it would in an experiment). At the moment, programs for circuit synthesis only exist in some special cases involving the synthesis of filters (the user program determines the model of the system from the imposed characteristics).

Simulation systems are also encountered in the area of process control, both in the analysis and the synthesis of systems (sequential process controllers, Petri nets, etc.).

CAD systems for electronics very often enable the mask for printed or integrated circuits to be defined from a theoretical model of the circuit being studied and thus to give it a realizable form. This is 'routeing', an application involving topological optimization.

In the classical case of the study of analogue systems, simulation generally permits three types of circuit investigation:

(1) *DC analysis* in which the steady DC state of the circuit is determined. The solution normally serves as an input to other analytical programs (AC or transient state) for calculating either the responses to variations around the DC operating point (harmonic analysis) or the behaviour starting from specified initial conditions (transient analysis).

(2) *AC or harmonic analysis*. If a sinusoidal signal of given frequency is applied to the circuit, the linear steady state can be determined (small

AC signals). It is also possible to carry out a frequency analysis to determine the frequency response curve of the circuit. This type of analysis involves the solution of systems of equations with complex magnitudes.

(3) *Transient analysis,* which enables the response of the circuit to be defined as a function of time when various signals specified by the user are applied to it. The solution is determined either from the imposed initial conditions or from the DC analysis. This analysis involves the solution of systems of non-linear equations.

Other methods of investigation are also provided by CAD in the electronics field. These are parametric analyses, generally using simulation, e.g.:

(1) *Studying the sensitivity of a circuit* (variations in the output magnitudes of a circuit when changes are made in a parameter).

(2) *Analysis of tolerances* (determination of nominal values for the circuit elements: the response envelope of the circuit is obtained when the various components are varied within the extreme limits of their values imposed by the tolerances).

(3) *Statistical (or Monte Carlo) analysis* (applied in the mass production of circuits: this program carries out an analysis of the system when its parameters are made to vary randomly within fixed tolerances).

Circuits are simulated using a representation of each of the elements of the system being studied. Each element therefore has to be associated with an equivalent circuit, called the 'model', characterized by its main parameters. The details incorporated in the model, i.e. the numbers of parameters used, depend upon the required accuracy.

The model chosen is thus a compromise between complexity and accuracy. In general, CAD has available a library of models for standard components such as resistors, capacitors, inductors, diodes, bipolar transistors, MOSFETs, etc. together with those for macromodels such as operational amplifiers.

A macromodel is a simplified model of a complex element (itself a modelled circuit) which has the same external behaviour as the real component, at least for a useful range of phenomena.

2.3.4 Computer-aided manufacturing

Making a model of the object using CAD provides a knowledge of the design constraints (shapes, surface areas, etc.) and this enables the manufacturing parameters to be calculated and passed on to the numerically controlled machine tools.

Computer-aided manufacturing (CAM) is the use of data-processing facilities to generate the data required for the numerically controlled machines, for robots and for process control. The technique also includes the task of simulating the manufacturing process (e.g. simulating the path of a tool during a machining operation).

In a more integrated approach, CAM also carries out the remote downloading of CAM programs on to directly NC (DNC) machines from the manufacturing program of the computer-based PIC system (see Sec. 3.3). When integrated with production control, CAM enables production schedules to be completed by the NC machine tool programs and thus makes it possible to coordinate the whole production or manufacturing process in the factory (Fig. 2.6).

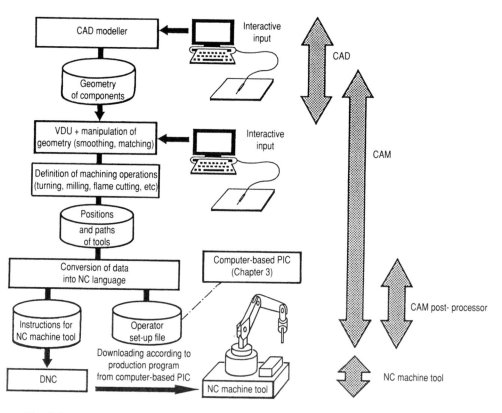

Fig. 2.6.
Integration of CAD and CAM.

CAM is used not only in the mechanical engineering industry but in the electronics industry as well, for example in mapping out printed circuit boards, in computer-controlled photolithography, in the automatic insertion of components, etc.

2.4 PRODUCTION CONTROL

Production control involves (1) planning the means required for the production process, and (2) controlling its execution. Its functions cover an enormous field, from the development of the medium- or long-term production programme to the monitoring of plant operations by covering all the coordinating activities such as defining the product structure (bills of materials, production schedules, etc.), stock control, material requirements planning (MRP), purchasing, workshop planning, etc.

The boundaries of computer-based PIC systems are not always very well defined. Thus, it is quite possible to consider that their responsibilities include the scheduling and supervision of workshop operations or, much further upstream, the development of the master schedule. Thus PIC systems are at the very heart of CIM and we shall therefore be examining them in greater detail in Chapter 3. A computer-based PIC system whose overall aim is to optimize the resources of the company (materials and costs) for a given volume of production uses two types of data:

(1) *Static data* representing the product structure (products, schedules, bills of materials, machines, suppliers, etc). These data are shared with the design/production stage (CAD system) and their handling is the responsibility of the methods section.

(2) *Dynamic data* consisting of the flow of information tapped by the production programme (customer orders, manufacturing orders, stock movements, time checks, etc.).

2.5 MANUFACTURING PLANT AND PRODUCTION SYSTEMS

The transfer lines in the car industry are an example of the integration of the production process dating from well before the advent of the CIM concept. At that time no flexibility was needed since the components generally had to be produced continuously and in very large numbers. These lines represented a high investment with limited flexibility (Henry Ford was said to be ready to supply Americans with 'a car of any colour,

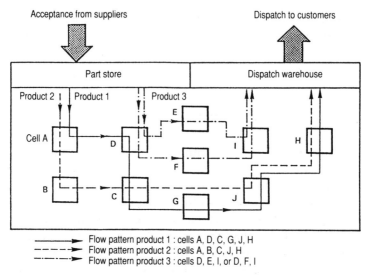

Fig. 2.7.
A flexible manufacturing system.

as long as it's black'). Present-day market pressures no longer allow such a luxury. On the contrary, the demands in quality and cost have become ever greater and the life cycle of products is increasingly uncertain.

We have already seen that a reorganization of workstations based on the flow of materials and parts instead of in homogeneous sections, as suggested by the advantages of specialization, can often reduce movement, storage and operational sequences in a manufacturing plant without the use of any avant-garde technology. This frequently brings considerable benefits in reducing lead times and work in progress.

However, such elementary organizational methods no longer enable modern manufacturing units to achieve the necessary responsiveness. New rules have arrived on the scene to guide the design of installations. What is being sought is net profitability from the means of production, even at a very low rate of use, together with the ability to reconfigure installations (during a change in production) very quickly and at minimal cost through the use of work centres or what are called *flexible manufacturing systems* (FMSs, Fig. 2.7).

An FMS is designed around autonomous cells, forming nodes in the production flow pattern. Such a system has three essential properties:

(1) it is automated;
(2) it is capable of manufacturing several types of product;

(3) the changeover from manufacturing one type of product to another is brief and is ideally carried out by overlapping of the operations.

An autonomous cell brings together the various automated means of production (such as a machining centre or NC machine tool, robot, palletizer, tool-changing carousel) which between them provide for the operational control of elementary functions using combined programs for execution and local handling. It is then possible to reconfigure the cell for various operations of a similar kind, such as milling, turning or surface treatment.

The automatic handling system in a flexible plant produces the item to be manufactured by passing it through the appropriate cells according to a production schedule.

2.5.1 Scheduling problems

In the field of production, scheduling problems appear in many areas, whether it is a question of evaluating performance in a future work centre, of programming the activities in an operational production plan or of simulating the behaviour of an existing production system when faced with a choice to be made at the strategic level.

Scheduling is programming the execution of production by allocating resources to tasks and fixing the times at which they are used. The data involved in such a problem are of four types:

(1) The *tasks* (or activities), characterized by their durations.

(2) The *potential constraints*, which are generally expressed by precedence constraints (activity B follows activity A) and time constraints (task A must be completed by a certain date or must not begin before a certain date). The set of potential constraints is modelled by a quantitative graph. Standard scheduling methods such as PERT (program evaluation and review technique) or CPA (critical path analysis) are based essentially on this type of graph.

(3) The *resources*, i.e. any goods or services essential for carrying out a task (machine, workforce, raw materials, finance, etc.). There are two types of resource (a) renewable resources which, after being allotted to a task are again available at the end of it for other tasks (machines, personnel), and (b) consumables which, after use, are no longer available (money, raw materials).

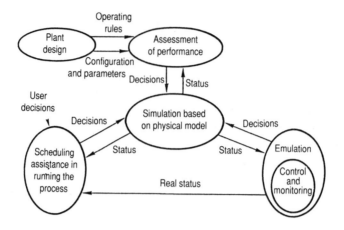

Fig. 2.8.
The areas covered by simulation in production systems.

(4) The *economic function* which, using several criteria, assesses the efficiency with which resources are used. In solving a scheduling problem at the same time as attempting to comply with time constraints it is necessary to optimize the use of certain resources, for example minimizing a particular cost, or minimizing the overall lead time.

Modern scheduling techniques are turning increasingly to interactive systems instead of the crude methods of the 1970s operating solely in batch mode. These techniques are now being increasingly used since they enable responses to be made that are in harmony with the demands on the responsiveness of production (a problem of scheduling short-term operational tasks may be solved in transactional mode by a plant manager, enabling priority tasks to be undertaken at once).

Interactive facilities intended as scheduling aids are not merely aimed at solving scheduling problems and thus seeking a set of possible solutions: they also allow the functioning of the system in question (workshop, process) to be simulated (Fig. 2.8). In this way they provide the operator with the possibility of exploring interesting scenarios which would have been excluded by the purely quantitative criteria of a computer program providing a numerical solution. Moreover, the modelling methods used in interactive systems provide a clear description of scheduling problems.

2.5.2   The maintenance of plant and of manufacturing systems

With the 'tightness' in production flow required in modern manufacturing organizations, the concept of equipment availability has become more

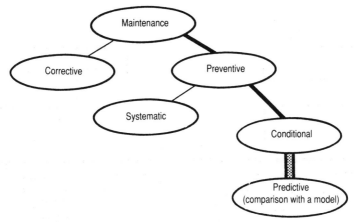

Fig. 2.9.
Development of the maintenance function.

crucial than ever. The philosophy of JIT production does not allow for the breakdown of machines.

The 'maintenance' function, whose mission is to keep plant in a specified condition or to bring it up to that condition so as to provide a given service, nowadays has a role that is more preventive than curative (Fig. 2.9).

The importance currently ascribed to the 'maintenance' function can be judged by the resources devoted to it. Its operating costs amount to between 4 and 15% of turnover and it employs between 3 and 30% of the total personnel. The stock available to it (pieceparts, tools) are often equivalent to 18 months' consumption. There are still few indicators of its effectiveness.

With the automation of manufacturing plants, the maintenance service has come into its own: to maintain a system one must be fully conversant with it, and since this is only possible with a complete knowledge of the system, information technology has become a major force in the accomplishment of maintenance tasks. Such tasks can be divided into the following:

(1) *Tasks which are mostly technical in nature*, i.e. accident prevention, data acquisition, diagnostic models, trouble-shooting, repairs and, upstream, the production of bills of materials and schedules.

(2) *Managerial tasks*, such as the management of documentation, of material resources (tools, measuring equipment), of personnel (staffing, workloads), records of breakdowns, budgeting, costing, etc.

Modern machines and equipment (NC machine tools, large motors, compressors, PLCs, etc.) are now fitted with local or central monitoring

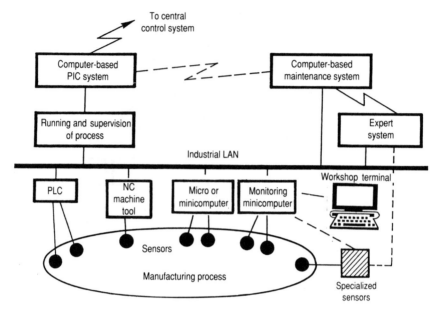

Fig. 2.10.
The structure of computer-aided maintenance.

systems forming the basis of a computer-aided maintenance structure (Fig. 2.10).

In a computer-aided maintenance system, a host computer monitors the production lines and records all that happens, thus forming a record from which it is possible to calculate the breakdown rate of the various pieces of equipment, the mean time before failure (MBTF), the mean time to repair (MTTR), etc.

Counters in the host-computer can then add up the number of cycles for the components and trigger an alarm when a tool change or change of component becomes necessary. This is the beginning of conditional maintenance.

The information gathered at this first level is sent to the following:

(1) The computer-aided maintenance control (CAMC) system, which centralizes the information and provides the 'management'-type functions (e.g. documentation, records of breakdowns, resources); a CAMC system can be regarded as the equivalent of a computer-based PIC system whose resources are the maintenance specialists, the tools and pieceparts and whose products are the tasks of maintenance and repair. Just as in production control, managing maintenance involves

the planning of activities and supplies (spare parts, tools), controlling costs, etc.

(2) Diagnostic aid systems: often regarded mistakenly as expert systems, these applications enable corrective action to be undertaken after symptoms have been observed, generally by using simulation.

(3) The quality control system, to monitor the path of incidents in a production batch and to provide information about corrective action to be undertaken in the process (see Sec. 3.5).

(4) Sometimes to the multi-media server, so as to facilitate trouble-shooting or the action to be taken by providing the specialist with the technical data files needed for such action (work sheets, dispatch warehouse dockets, diagrams, plans, photographs, operational files, etc.).

It is clear that, in a CIM environment, basic technical data such as bills of materials, schedules, workstations, etc. dealt with by computer-aided maintenance will be held in common with the computer-based PIC system (see Sec. 3.2).

2.6   COMMUNICATION BETWEEN APPLICATIONS

The first data-processing structures encountered in manufacturing industry were star networks around a host computer. Today there is a wide range of equipment in the typical manufacturing plant: robots, programmable logic controllers (PLCs), various terminals (some dedicated), microcomputers and minicomputers, each with their own 'intelligence' and store of local data. Providing a means of communication between these diverse systems is thus a major factor in improving the integration of functions. One of the main aims of CIM is to support and coordinate exchanges of information between applications.

A standard way of representing a company divides its functions into five levels (Fig. 2.11). Within each level, horizontal communication is provided through a local network. Vertical communication between two adjacent levels is provided by a gateway system between two local networks (e.g. the company LAN and the factory LAN are coupled in the functional sense by the production control system).

We thus arrive at a distributed structure for the company's information system (Fig. 2.12). Each application or information system (we shall call it a node) which communicates within the system will most often have its own store of local data. Integrating the data at the company level requires

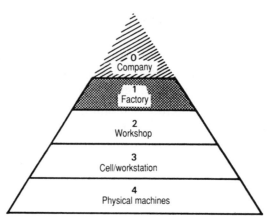

Fig. 2.11.
The hierarchical structure of a company.

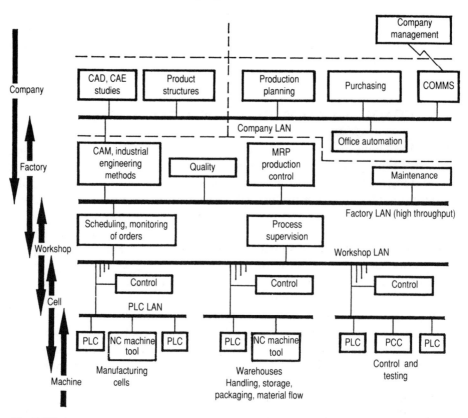

Fig. 2.12.
The structure of a management information system. COMMS = interface with external networks; PCC = production control computer; PLC = programmable logic controller.

a knowledge of the possible ways in which the various elements can communicate with each other and it also means complying with a new distribution procedure.

Implementing this procedure involves the widest possible study of the set of applications to be integrated (conceptual models of communication, of data and of processes—see Sec. 6.2) so that each item of information is stored only once in the most appropriate system (using criteria related to access, security of information and processing times—see Sec. 5.3.3).

The LAN world, particularly that of industrial LANs, has long suffered from being restricted to a very closed set of proprietary networks. Faced with the large number of international standards (ISO and CCITT) capable of being adapted for these networks, users decided to make themselves mutually comprehensible through two groups:

(1) MAP (Manufacturing Automation Protocol), launched by General Motors and concerned with standardization of industrial LANs.
(2) TOP (Technical and Office Protocol), set up on the initiative of Boeing and concerned with scientific and office LANs.

These two projects have now resulted in a user standard based on the seven-layer ISO model (MAP 3.0 standard). This standard only operates at present (beginning of 1989) at the factory level.

The field of industrial LANs is still covered by the hybrid standards of proprietary suppliers. The MiniMAP standard is being developed with the aim of providing a norm in this field.

Towards a new type of management

The effects of the Taylor system and the division of responsibility extend to the highest levels of the organizational flow chart. During a recent inquiry in a large company, 90% of the engineers and technical managers questioned considered that the essential mission of the company today was to produce. Only 10% replied that it was to 'sell'.

The establishment of an integrated structure for all the information systems in a company will be accompanied by a change in professional behaviour. It encourages decentralization of decision-making and thus contributes to the dismantling of large subdivided organizations inherited from the years of growth. The ossified pyramidal model will be abandoned in favour of an approach more closely related to the multicellular structure (Fig. 2.13) typical of biological structures and the life sciences, whose responsive, adaptive and creative properties are well known.

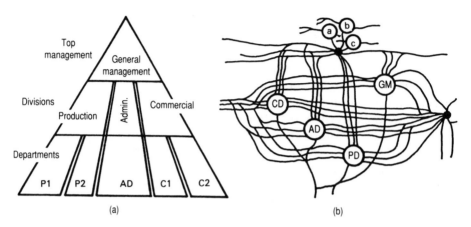

(a)   (b)

Fig. 2.13.
Management structures: (a) the pyramid structure in which each department is considered to be a miniature enterprise and the channels of communication must follow vertical paths between the hierarchical levels; (b) the multicellular structure, in which communication takes place freely between different levels and different specialisms. Vertical lines of communication are not enforced when the progress of the company is involved.

This model, which cyberneticists liken to the image of neurons in the human brain, is based on an infrastructure and on modes of communication similar to those in the CIM model. Through this new approach, it will become possible for large and medium-scale companies to gain access to a form of organization that is particularly effective but so far reserved to small enterprises: that of the craft worker.

A profound social phenomenon is also created by abundance: work is no longer undertaken merely to provide for material needs, but also to satisfy everybody's demands for the right to fulfilment and personal growth in their professional occupations. In contrast, many of the jobs created by the Taylor system do not lend themselves to such a development.

The implementation of a CIM structure leads to the decentralization of operational decisions and provides every level with the possibility of selective access to information. We see a higher value being placed on the workforce, particularly production staff, by giving them responsibility. CIM methods will facilitate the introduction of a modern form of management which relies on the indispensable participation of workers and a reduction in the number of hierarchical levels in order to allow companies to evolve in an uncertain future by improving their performance as regards responsiveness, flexibility and creativity. One large French firm has reduced the number of hierarchical levels in this way from seven to five, and has restructured its 104 divisions into 600 autonomous groups.

In an excessively automated world, can we still accept the under-exploitation of skills and abilities to the point where the company is deprived of the fantastic reasoning powers of some human brains, whose faculties will undoubtedly always be superior to those of the machine? Victor Hugo claimed that work 'would make Apollo a hunchback, and Voltaire a cretin'. CIM is one of the tools which will surely improve working conditions to levels far above the subhuman ones implied by that quotation, since the added value contributed by workers to the production process will become mainly intellectual.

3   Integrated Production Control: the Backbone of CIM

3.1   ON THE IMPORTANCE OF AN INTEGRATED SYSTEM OF PRODUCTION CONTROL

The integration of the production process is achieved in a CIM context by setting up an information structure which carries the flow of data to any part of the system (see Sec. 5.1). The establishment of such a structure will rely on an industrial database providing for the overall integration of the company's technical and economic data.

A computer-based system of production and inventory control (PIC) has the specific function of managing the manpower and material resources of an industrial company in such a way as to produce the best compromise between three contradictory objectives at any moment. These objectives are as follows:

(1) *Commercial*: maximum customer service and hence large stocks and great flexibility.
(2) *Financial*: minimum immobilization of workforce and materials, and minimum work in progress.
(3) *Production-related*: maximum efficiency in the use of manufacturing resources through longer runs and production in larger batches.

Almost the whole company will be involved in attaining these objectives, so that the production control system must be supported by a database providing a detailed and faithful model of the variables describing the state of the company.

The database, which is the core of the PIC system, will also provide information to all the other industrial applications in the company (CAD, process supervision, CAM, business management, etc.) and will guarantee

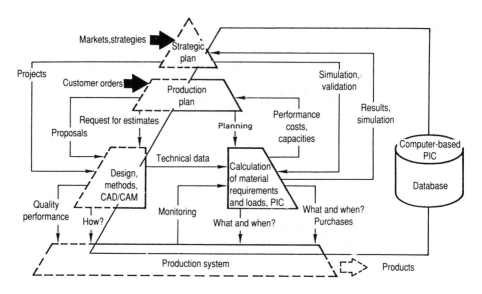

Fig. 3.1
The production control system.

the integrity of all the data (no redundant data and data available in real time).

Production control may be considered to include the following tasks (Fig. 3.1):

(1) programming of manufacturing requirements and requirements of the purchasing division;
(2) analysis of loads and capacities, of availability and feasibility (lead times);
(3) stock control policy;
(4) scheduling and release of manufacturing orders;
(5) technical documentation;
(6) monitoring of progress in production.

It should be pointed out that the calculation of the return on investment in a computer-based PIC system should nowadays take into account not only such aspects as the quality of service, the stocks and direct productivity but also, and more importantly, the unified nature of the flow of information. The latter is measured by the quality and productivity of personnel engaged in indirect activities, and by the flexibility of the whole company and the way it is managed. Many examples can be quoted to show that profits are not always made if only those criteria involving stocks, lead times and direct productivity are considered, but that there is always an improvement when a global view is taken, and this is in line with the synergy promoted by CIM.

We are concerned in this chapter with the classic concepts of production control originating in MRP2 systems, i.e. systems which deal with all the processes taking place in a company.

3.2   FORMAL STRUCTURE OF THE TECHNICAL DATA IN AN INDUSTRIAL COMPANY

Product structure, manufacturing processes, costs, etc. need to be defined and monitored at the level of the various interacting sections (such as production, purchasing, sales administration, etc.). In order to do this we adopt a formal structure for the technical data involved in production, based on the four features given under the headings below.

(a)   Items

In line with the AFNOR* standard X 60-012, *'Terms and definitions of the constitutive elements and their supplies for consumer durables'*, we define an item as 'a good identified as such, forming an element of the bill of materials or catalogue'. It therefore concerns all the products or components made use of in the company, e.g. raw materials, marketed items, supplies, subcontracted items, manufactured sub-assemblies. Each of these items should have its own unique reference number.

(b)   Bill of materials

A bill of materials forms a tree structure which represents the way in which the components are related to each other in making up the composite finished product.

Example. Figure 3.2 shows the structure of a four-level bill of materials for a cosmetic with total or partial continuous-flow production, intermediate stocks, standard or common sub-assemblies.

The number of levels in a bill of materials depends on the way the production is organized. Thus, after the packaging of the carton in Fig. 3.2 has been incorporated into the flow-line production system, the number

---

*AFNOR = Association Française de Normalisation, the French standards institute.

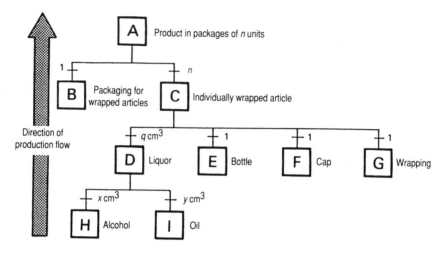

Fig. 3.2
A bill of materials with a four-level structure.

of levels in the bill of materials could be changed from four to three (Fig. 3.3). Formally, we should say that there had been an improvement in the integration of the production process.

(c)   Production schedules

Production schedules describe the manufacturing process or the operational procedure, i.e. the ordered set of operations to be carried out in

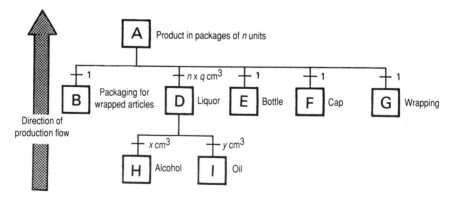

Fig. 3.3
Reduction of the product structure in Fig. 3.2 to three levels.

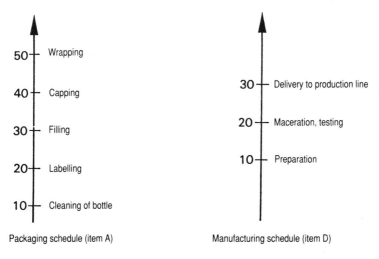

Packaging schedule (item A)   Manufacturing schedule (item D)

Fig. 3.4.
Typical production schedules.

order to pass from one level of the bill of materials to the level immediately above.

The production schedules for the products A and D in Figs 3.2 and 3.3 could be illustrated as in Fig. 3.4. Each operation is defined by its work-station, the parameters involved in its completion time (preparation time, rate of execution, transfer time, waiting time), the skill of the workforce and so on.

(d) Means of production and workstations

In very general terms, we understand by 'means of production' the set of manufacturing resources, factors or agents available to the company for the transformation of goods and services into manufactured products. Such means therefore include the machines, tools, warehouses and work-shops, as well as the subcontractors and the employees. Materials are considered as a special factor since they are consumable or created resources and form part of the data under 'items'.

In this connection, when a decision is made that something should not be considered as a 'means of production', it must be brought under specific control (e.g. manpower, handling facilities). In the simplest case, the means of production will be:

(1) workstations related to the activity;

(2) logical groupings of the means of production (e.g. factories, work-shops, departments, work centres, warehouses).

and a workstation will then be defined by (a) its code and description, (b) its links (geographical and accounting), (c) its capacity (e.g. number of machines and operators, operating schedule) and (d) its rating.

3.3 MRP AND MRP2

The role of computer-based PIC is to manage the material resources and loads with the requirement that a reduction in stocks, an increase in productivity and an improvement in the quality of service should all be optimized simultaneously.

The PIC system is generally run with three or even four different planning horizons:

(1) *In the very long term*, the system will set up the master production schedule (MPS) which, in terms of certain parameters (customer orders, sales forecasts, stocks and workloads) associated with strategic data and large-scale production schedules, makes it possible to simulate the future direction of a company in terms of a *production strategy* and an *organization*.

(2) The forecasts or actual items ordered by customers will constitute the requirements for a *medium-term* production programme making it possible to set up *supplies of materials* and a *planning of workloads at infinite capacity* (i.e. with no account being taken of the real capacity of the workstations; the workloads relating to each manufacturing order will thus be spread over time without any account being taken of competing workloads).

(3) *In the short term*, workshop scheduling will make it possible to plan the workloads week by week, or even day by day, taking into account the actual capacities of the workstations and the production priorities.

(4) Finally, monitoring a plant *in real time* will enable the validity of the assumptions made upstream to be checked and, if necessary, corrected (*feedback* or regulation of a system using a closed loop). It is then possible to analyse the differences between time taken and time allo-cated (a function of the methods office) and those between standard costs and real costs (a function of business management).

The overall approach embodied in these principles was developed around a basic concept whose origins go back to 1965, known as Material

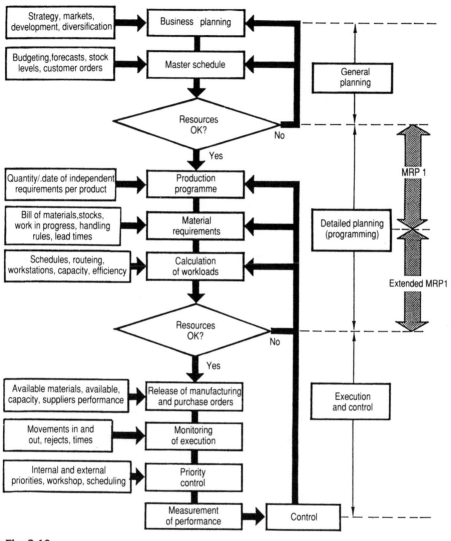

Fig. 3.10.
Flow chart for MRP2.

3.4 THE TRUTH ABOUT PRODUCTION COSTS

As in the similar case of the reduction in lead times, it is now no longer reasonable to produce anything without a complete knowledge of the economic bases of manufacturing.

The production control system, by using either prior estimates or real assessments made after manufacture, contributes to the measurement, and

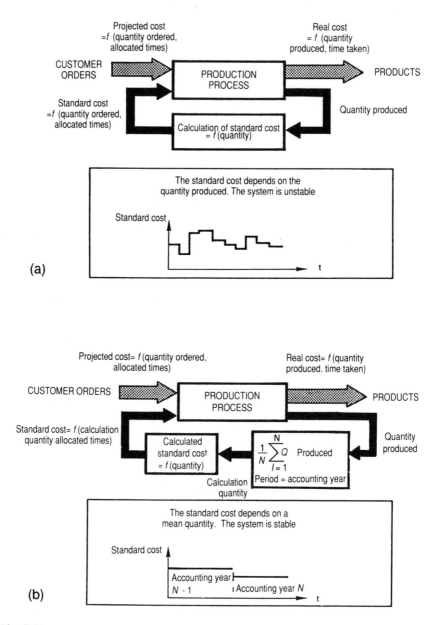

Fig. 3.11.
(a) Calculation of standard cost without integral correction; (b) with integral correction.

hence the control, of profitability. It does this classically by dealing with three types of cost per item (we understand by 'item' the meaning given in Sec. 3.2, i.e. raw materials, products in process of manufacture within the operational cycle, supplies already received or finished products). These are as follows:

(1) *The standard cost* of the article, an accounting basis defined over a given period.

(2) *The projected cost* of an article for a given order, which will depend directly on the quantity produced.

(3) *The real cost* of the article in a manufacturing order, measured after its completion.

The standard and projected costs are two *a priori* estimates made in the context of a traditional MRP2 system by implosion of the bill of materials, a mechanism we describe in detail later.

The projected cost is therefore determined on the basis of the quantity in the manufacturing order, the unit costs of the articles supplied and elementary data on the added value (labour costs, cost of machine time, time taken).

Because of its dependence on scale (i.e. the quantities made) the projected cost will be specific to each manufacturing order. However, the constraints on the management of the company (e.g. price structure, analytical accounting, budgets) mean that it must work with constant values over a fixed period. We are therefore led to define the standard cost (or prior assessment) as a projected cost calculated on the basis of an average quantity. This cost will be updated at a predetermined frequency, generally the accounting year.

Once again, systems theory shows us that the stability of the production process and costs is determined by the parameters with large time constants (allocated times, costs, quantities used for the purposes of calculation). This method of costing using a mean value over a given period is called 'integral correction' (Fig. 3.11(a) and (b)).

3.4.1 Determination of the overall cost of a product

Overall cost covers everything that has contributed to the cost of the product when it has reached the final stage of its progress through the company, including its distribution. It is thus a quantity that only concerns products that are sold. In calculating an overall cost, the following have to be determined in turn:

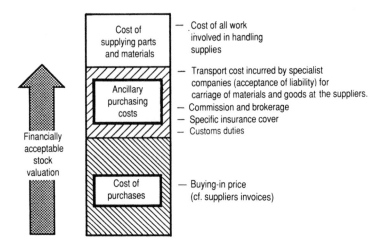

Fig. 3.12.
Breakdown of purchasing costs.

(1) The cost of purchasing raw materials and supplies.
(2) The cost of producing the finished article emerging from the machine shops.
(3) The overall cost of the product, i.e. its production costs increased by the corresponding marketing costs.

Purchasing costs include the total amounts occurring in the suppliers' invoices, ancillary purchasing expenses and costs associated with the supply of parts and materials (Fig. 3.12).
The overall cost (Fig. 3.13) includes the following:

(1) The production cost (i.e. the cost of purchasing raw materials, supplies and services used, to which are added other costs borne by the company during manufacture).
(2) Costs excluding production costs, consisting of distribution costs and a proportion of the general administrative costs, financial charges and R & D costs, particularly for any general research undertaken.

The concept of *price* is often mistakenly used and should be clearly distinguished from that of cost. Price is the monetary expression of the value of a transaction upstream (purchase price) or downstream (selling price) and the term therefore only applies to the relationships between the company and the outside world.

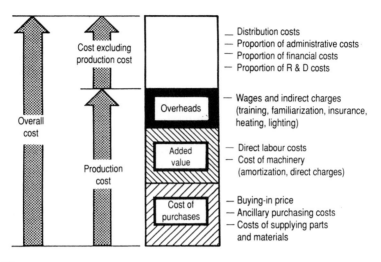

Fig. 3.13.
Breakdown of overall cost.

3.4.2   Determination of cost by implosion of the bill of materials

The structure of the data in an MRP2 system (items, schedules, bills of materials and the network of orders) lends itself very well to the mechanics of the price-fixing process recommended by modern analytical accounting methods.

The method of calculation by implosion of the bill of materials involves starting from the components at the lowest level (materials supplied), determining the production cost for the series of composite articles and working up to the highest level, i.e. the finished product.

To do this, we first establish the aggregate cost of the materials for the first composite sub-assembly formed, i.e. the sum of the costs of the direct components. The added value and overheads (indirect charges) are then calculated from the scheduling data. The sum of the aggregate material costs, the added value and the overheads thus forms the production costs for the first manufactured sub-assembly.

This procedure is then repeated at the next level up, and so on, until the last level, the material costs being the basic production costs for each of the sub-assemblies. The cost determined on the last component, i.e. the finished product, then corresponds to the production cost of the marketed article in the classical sense of the term.

The method can be applied in the same way to the calculation of standard costs (where the quantity dividing the fixed expenses in the calculation is a standard quantity established over the whole of the accounting year and where the times are the theoretical times allowed for in the production schedules); and to the calculation of projected costs for a particular order (the quantity used in the calculation is the ordered quantity and the times are those allocated theoretically).

The real costs obtained after the manufacturing process has occurred and has been checked are also 'assembled' by this method. This time the quantity used in the calculation is the quantity produced for the manufacturing order (manual or automatic weighing or counting) and the times are the times actually taken, checked off on the integrated monitoring system (a check-off of the work slips at the beginning and end of operations on bar-code terminals or with magnetic badges).

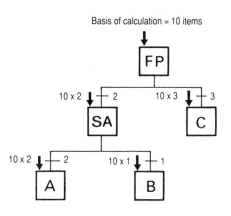

Fig. 3.14.
Product structure for a finished product FP with a two-level bill of materials.

To illustrate the method, consider the example shown in Fig. 3.14, where FP is a finished product and the bill of materials has two levels. The quantity of finished product used in the calculation is either the quantity ordered (in the case of a projected cost) or the quantity based on a the calculation of the fixed standard cost for the article. We begin by determining the production cost of the components in the lowest level (in the present case, the sub-assembly, SA). In this way, we establish the accumulated material costs (costs of direct components) and the direct added-value cost supplemented by indirect charges or production expenses (worked out from the scheduling data and from general technical data) (Fig. 3.15). This value is then allocated to the first product, SA, as the cost of materials component and the procedure is repeated at the higher level, i.e. on the finished product FP (Fig. 3.16).

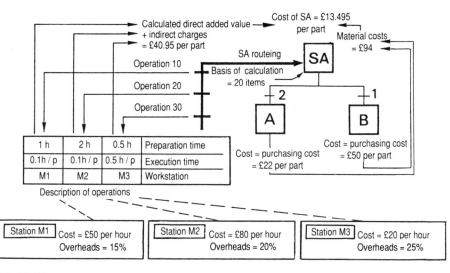

Fig. 3.15.
Calculation of costs for the sub-assembly SA of Fig. 3.14.

The basic importance of this method is that, if any changes occur in the price or the production process or if there are any modifications of technical data, they can be taken into account at any time at all levels, and are thus included in the overall cost of the finished article. To do this, we only have to repeat the implosion process over the products involved.

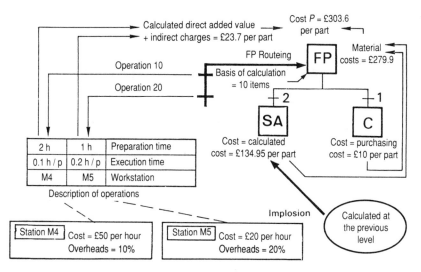

Fig. 3.16.
Calculation of costs for the finished product FP of Fig. 3.14.

3.5   ORDER TRACKING AS SUPPORT FOR QUALITY CONTROL

The concept of quality in the production process can be viewed in terms of a chain whose strength is that of the weakest link, in accordance with reliability theory.

The characteristics of the chain do not remain the same as time goes on. The position of the weak link or links fluctuates from one item to another. It is then necessary to monitor each product or batch of products and attach to it a record of its state or of all the events that occur during the production process.

This amounts to creating a flow of information moving parallel to the flow of production, to which a set of variables describing the states are assigned during the manufacture of the product. Within an MRP2 system, such a stream of information is established in order to monitor production. This involves the acquisition or measurement of data on quantities and times (forming an information 'vector') which will allow the production control system to be regulated through a closed feedback loop. A quantitative information vector of this type could easily be supplemented by one carrying a set of qualitative data on the state of the production process using the same data acquisition facilities (Fig. 3.17).

We can explain this method of quality checks more clearly by looking at the scenario of an MRP2 production system in a simple case (Fig. 3.18). Suppose there is an order for a quantity Q of the product FP (items ordered or sales forecast) for the date t. The calculation of the net requirements will generate orders for the various components (Fig. 3.19). The unpredictable

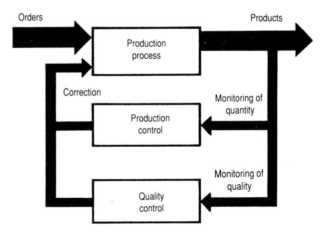

Fig. 3.17.
Flow of information in a quality-control system.

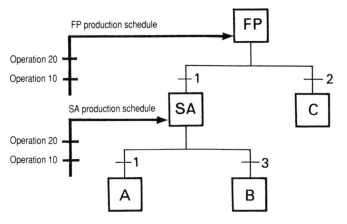

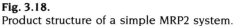

Fig. 3.18.
Product structure of a simple MRP2 system.

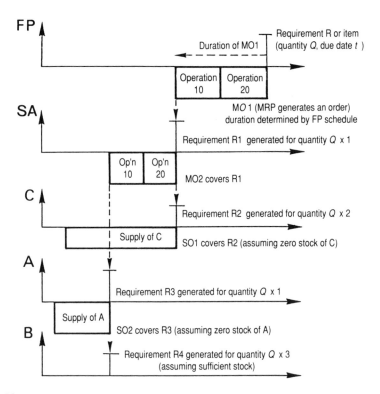

Fig. 3.19.
Generation of orders in the system of Fig. 3.18. MO = manufacturing order, SO = supply order.

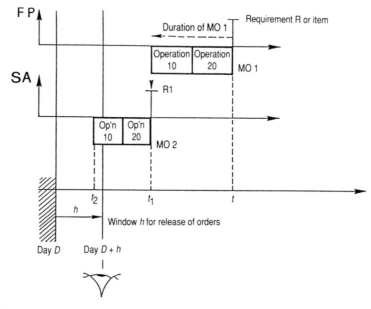

Fig. 3.20.
Time-scale for the orders generated in Fig. 3.19.

nature of consumption, i.e. frequent changes in the forecast of market demand, will be reflected in almost permanent upheavals in the order books, both for manufacturing and supplies.

To fix an order, in quantity or in date, by external manual intervention effectively removes one degree of freedom from the planning system. The more the orders are locked, the more complicated are the problems involved in calculating the requirements and timing the orders, and hence the further we shall be from an optimum outcome.

In Fig. 3.20 t_2 is the date at which manufacture of the sub-assemblies SA starts, and h is the forecast date for the release of orders. From $D + h$ ($\geq t_2$), the controller of article SA will be able to release the order MO2, having previously taken care to verify the availability of the direct components A and B. The release will take place, at the latest, when its manufacture begins (t_2).

Confirmation of a manufacturing order means that the components and the resources of the plant (machines, operators, tools) can be reserved for the operations in line with a short-term schedule. The vector carrying the information on quality will then be created with the initial conditions for fulfilling the order (machine reference, serial numbers of operators, tool numbers, etc.). The data contained in this vector depend on predeter-

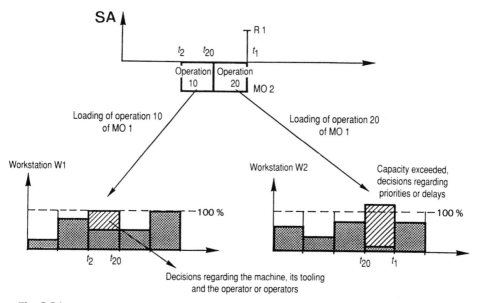

Fig. 3.21.
Use of allocated resources in the operation of Fig. 3.20.

mined parameters (scheduling information) and on random circumstances (availability of resources) (Fig. 3.21).

Note that, in a CIM context, the initiation of the order by the workshop schedule system may trigger the remote loading of programs into NC machine tools and robots from the CAM system.

The manufacturing order will then be carried out in accordance with the scheduling instructions. Data on the quantities made and the times taken for each of the monitored operations will be fed to the system by means of job shop terminals (e.g. bar code scanner, 'hard' keyboard, badge reader) or sensors of physical quantities (e.g. weighing scales, piece counters). Such data acquisition devices can also be used to send the sequence of qualitative events to the system (e.g. parameters of adjustments made, any malfunctioning recorded). The manufacturing order may be considered as the factor that unifies the information gained from monitoring a batch of products.

Since a finished product very often involves several levels of the bill of materials, the continuity of the information from the monitoring of one batch can only be guaranteed if the orders from successive levels of the bill of materials are matched up. This process, which involves *marking* each order with its child and parent orders (when they exist), is the origin of the property we call *order tracking* in the MRP2 system.

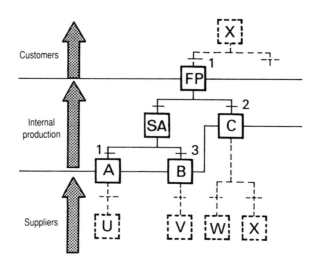

Fig. 3.22.
Product structure in an extended bill of materials (including suppliers and customers).

In the above example, the information vector for monitoring the production process is formed from the complete set of entries in the manufacturing orders (MO1 and MO2) and supply orders (SO1, SO2 and SO3) which are concerned with checking.

The method can easily be generalized to the chain of suppliers upstream and customers downstream (in the case of production for an industrial customer) (Fig. 3.22). The interfaces in such an *extended bill of materials* are handled by value-added networks (see Sec. 2.6).

The main providers of orders are the large car manufacturers. This sector is now pressurizing its suppliers to *unify their information technology systems*. The aim of the ODETTE data exchange standard is the automation of customer/supplier circuits both in the control and coordination of the requirements and in the extended monitoring of quality. This standard is at present a major concern of all industrialists involved in automobile subcontracting and should be completely operational in the very near future.

In this way, when a product is observed not to behave in accordance with specifications, the demands of the market are making it possible to go back over the whole production chain as far as the preparation of raw materials in order to correct the process. As an example, suppose that a malfunction in the engines of a certain number of cars is traced back to a common batch of subcontracted parts. By examining the sequence of data on quality upstream of the supplier concerned, we might hypothetically find some abnormality in the casting process at the foundry.

The method is also of great interest to the pharmaceutical industry, where the sector involved in distribution to the general public has developed a similar standard for exchanges between suppliers with the GENCOD system. We can well imagine that such corporate standards will at some time in the future converge to a single standard.

4   Just-in-time
Production Systems

4.1 MAKE-TO-ORDER PRODUCTION

Maslow wrote in 1954 that human needs can be classified into five categories, forming a hierarchy with bare survival at the bottom and self-fulfilment at the top. Needs at the lower levels must be broadly satisfied before people become concerned about higher things.

The 'trade war' indulged in by companies in the developed world from the 1950s onwards made a great contribution to the increase in living standards of consumers. As a result, their needs experienced a considerable shift towards categories at the upper levels.

By the 1970s, the demands arising from the need for survival and security (the lower levels defined by Maslow) had been completely satisfied. Consumers' requirements had even passed beyond the stage where they arose from membership of a social group and had reached those associated with success and self-fulfilment. Relentless competition on an international scale ended up by making the consumer a 'spoilt child' whose whims then had to be gratified.

For industrialists, keeping or increasing their market share meant that they had to anticipate consumer demands. To achieve that, not only had they to supply products of an impeccable quality but they had also to cope with the fickle tastes of consumers which meant ever shorter useful lives for the products. It then became very risky to maintain stocks of finished articles, or of those in process of manufacture, which the unpredictable nature of the market might render obsolete at any moment.

Being competitive today mainly requires a capacity to anticipate or react quickly to new consumer needs, but it also depends on diversifying the list of marketed products (i.e. greater ranges of colour, presentation, packaging). The latter aspect is particularly important in sectors where the products are technically more 'stable', such as domestic electrical appliances and cars. For example, Matsushita increased the number of colours offered on its basic range of Panasonic refrigerators from 4 to 10 in 1983 and raised its sales by a factor of 1.5 over previous levels.

Such a proliferation of entries in trade catalogues has become totally incompatible with the idea of holding stocks of goods. Traditional production methods depend on the assumption that the manufacture of a new item requires a lead time and involves high start-up costs that impose the need for economic batches both in production and supply. If the organization of production is changed in such a way as to make the lead times and start-up costs negligible, this assumption becomes invalid and the idea of an economic order quantity loses its meaning. The quantity manufactured is then merely what is asked for by the customer and production only begins when the need arises.

More precisely:

(1) If the start-up cost becomes negligible, the idea of an economic order quantity loses all meaning: it is then possible to calculate the requirements in a completely logical way and only make the quantity strictly necessary.

(2) If the manufacturing lead time becomes negligible, it is then no longer necessary to set up sophisticated planning methods, since it is the observation of need which triggers the start of manufacture. Such a system can then be managed by using a 'reconstitution of consumption' method, such as the Kanban system.

4.2   REDUCING WASTAGE AND SIMPLIFYING

In a philosophical sense, the just-in-time (JIT) principle is summarized by 'produce the necessary quantity at the right moment'. A fundamental condition in attaining such an objective in practical terms is the *elimination of wastage* of any sort. Very often considerable stocks are present throughout the production process and allow latent problems to be concealed (Fig. 4.1). Among these are (1) production in batches or in runs imposed by a lack of flexibility in the machine tools, or (2) faults, rejects and breakdowns due to worn-out machines and inefficient processes. The reduction of stocks to levels that are related to the 'tightness' in the production flow will undoubtedly reveal such problems.

In the JIT approach, all activities or equipment contributing no added value to the product (waiting times, transit, storage) are considered as wastage and must be eliminated. It is thus a matter of manufacturing with the minimum of materials and equipment, and with the minimum amount

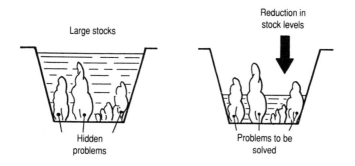

Fig. 4.1.
Illustrating the philosophy of JIT systems. Holding large stocks conceals some of the real underlying problems.

of space and time occupied by employees. The approach can be expressed in what may be called a 'five zeros' attitude:

(1) zero stock (production being 'pulled' by consumption throughout the process

(2) zero lead time (no waiting, reduction in transit times and in setting up times);

(3) zero faults (no longer accepting a statistical threshold of tolerated rejects);

(4) zero breakdowns (reliability of equipment ensured by preventive maintenance);

(5) zero paper (drastic simplification of administrative procedures).

It is worth pointing out that, in a JIT production process, it is not the systems (MRP or Kanban) which bring the maximum benefits, but rather the set of activities grouped mainly under *waste elimination* and *simplification*, together with improvements in the production system which make it more flexible. At Toyota, it has been said that 80% of the gains are due to elimination of waste, 15% to the development of the production system and 5% to the concept of production control, Kanban in this case.

4.3 CONTINUOUS-FLOW MANUFACTURING

Producing only on demand, i.e. without stocks and without lead times, is reflected in a continuously flowing production process, with a flow rate adjusted solely to that of the consumption (we then speak of a *pull system*

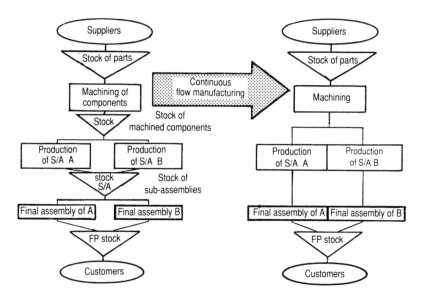

Fig. 4.2.
Continuous-flow manufacturing by reduction of intermediate stocks.

in contrast to a *push system*, where the production rate is determined by the nominal capacity of the critical items of manufacturing equipment).

In such a system, internal disruptions in the production flow must be as imperceptible as possible to the consumer. To that end, the procedures are formalized and the equipment is so arranged that it simulates the dynamics of fluid flow as closely as possible.

With this in mind, it is easy to see why it is important that the JIT concept should always be associated with total quality control TQC. It is because the objective is the maximum 'tightness' in the production flow: if any statistical reject rate were allowed, it would introduce a 'bubble' effect in the process which, in formal analogy with fluid mechanics, would 'de-energize' the production process.

Continuous-flow manufacturing makes it possible to avoid the build-up of stocks at intermediate levels of manufacture or assembly (Fig. 4.2). In this way, we avoid sub-assemblies in stock awaiting final assembly. The system known as the *two-level bill of materials* or the *indented bill of materials* depends on this idea.

The development from a traditional production process to a JIT system will be brought about by a change in the environment and a change in the management information system (MIS).

As regards the reorganization of the environment:

(1) competing resources in a traditional system become dedicated ones in JIT (tools, warehouses, equipment);

(2) production previously organized in machine shops is reconfigured into lines,

(3) new types of machine tool (machining centres, CNC machine tools) allow rapid tool-changing and avoid the resultant set-up times.

If we are more particularly concerned with the transition from a classical MRP system to an MRP/JIT system, the development at the MIS level is characterized by the following:

(1) a transition from production controlled by manufacturing orders to production controlled by a daily program;

(2) a restructuring of bills of materials by compressing intermediate levels (reducing stocks) (see Sec. 3.2);

(3) an 'on-stream' service of components, i.e. continuous at each operation and not an output of components from a single stock for the whole production of a batch as is required in a classical system.

4.3.1   Reducing and eliminating inter-operational transit

The basic rule of a JIT production system could be summarized by the statement that the aim is 'to honour every order from the consumer by immediate production (objective zero stock) within a very wide potential range of products'. Note that the idea of a consumer is generalized to any entity capable of calling for a finished or intermediate product (e.g. workshop, unit, ordering customers themselves working for an end consumer).

The above rule is being obeyed if the objective being pursued is to make the unit completion time of each product negligible. When the production is considered as a unit in this way, the time devoted to straightforward manufacturing represents only a few per cent of the overall lead time (see Sec. 1.4.2) and hence reduces the problem to minimizing the 'constant' components in this lead time (set-up time, tool-changing or tool reconfiguration time, waiting time, transit time).

Waiting times are often associated with the idea of holding intermediate stocks and, in a conventional organization, often form the largest proportion of the completion time. The JIT philosophy, by its very nature, enables such waiting times to be considerably 'compressed' by using continuous-flow manufacturing.

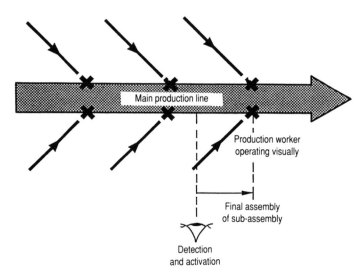

Fig. 4.3.
The 'herring-bone' type of production line.

Nevertheless, it is essential to make sure that the production line is kept in balance through the use of a synchronizing mechanism capable of avoiding any shortage of components in the line, while minimizing the size of the stock and the quantity of in-process products.

A simple example of such a technique of synchronization is that of the 'herring-bone' production line (Fig. 4.3). Each side bone is dedicated to the production of one type of sub-assembly (automatic or optional). It is obvious that a model as simplistic as this reflects only a very limited vision of the synchronization problems in JIT production. In general, the method applies only to lines used for the assembly of finished products.

It is very clear that the dismantling of homogeneous sections and the reorganization of machines into multi-functional units favours the rapid flow of products in workshops and hence contributes directly to a reduction in transit times.

In a less direct way, stock reduction also very often leads to a reduction in transit times. This is because the tendency with large stocks is to use common areas for them to save space. But the routes they have to take are then even longer and, in addition, handling often becomes complex and hence takes more time. The principle of *dedicated sites and dedicated resources* is of fundamental importance in optimizing the lengths of time taken up by inter-operational transit.

4.3.2   Reduction in tool-changing times: the SMED system

While the idea of eliminating waiting time and reducing transit times is an essential condition for the flexibility required by JIT organizations, quite as vital is a reduction in the time taken for setting up and reconfiguration of machines when there are changes in production.

The *single minute exchange of dies* (SMED) system, which we owe to the Japanese expert Shigeo Shingo, groups together a set of techniques which are easy to assimilate and enable a substantial reduction in tool-changing times to be achieved (from several hours to a few minutes).

The method involves four stages:

(1) Distinction between internal tasks which immobilize the machine, and external tasks which can be carried out while the machine is running. Note that a video system, even one that is relatively unsophisticated, turns out to be of enormous use in this type of task, particularly in facilitating timing operations.

(2) Transfer of internal tasks to external setting up procedures in order to maximize external tasks. This involves the development of an operational process for the setting up, in which certain tasks normally carried out when the machine is stopped will be carried out while it is running.

   The principle can be illustrated by the following example (Fig. 4.4): traditionally, the operator carries out all (or most) of the necessary steps while the machine is stopped. After a partial transfer of the internal tasks to external ones, the operational process could take on the structure shown in the example of Fig. 4.5.

   The operator asks for help some time before the end of the production in progress by actuating a simple flashing light installed on the machine (an Andon beacon is used in Japanese production units). The

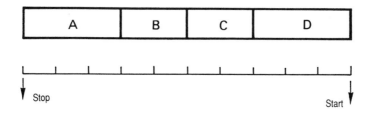

Fig. 4.4.
An internal set of tasks needs the machine to be stopped while they are carried out.

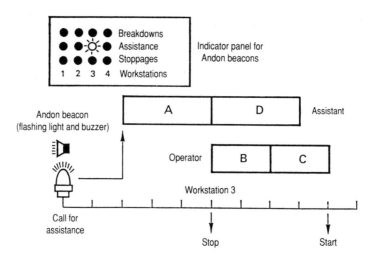

Fig. 4.5.
Application of the SMED method in which some internal tasks are turned into external ones which can be carried out while the machine is running.

request is relayed by a buzzer and an indicator lamp on a central table which calls on a team of 'flying' assistants. Tasks A and D are carried out in parallel by an assistant and the operator has only to carry out B (remove old tool) and C (set up new tool).

(3) The third step involves reducing the internal tasks by rationalizing all aspects of the setting-up operations (e.g. simplification of mountings, ergonomic studies).

(4) Finally, the same rationalization is applied to the external tasks, which may have less effect on lead times but nevertheless play a predominant part in the costs of setting up. This means undertaking a study of suitable methods of tool-handling, examining all aspects of clamping the tools and above all defining the sites dedicated to the various tools.

Note that priority is given to the reduction in operator waiting times at the expense of an increase in machine running time, thus leading to surplus production capacity. Using Toyota as an example once more: here, one person is in charge of five machines.

The cheapest possible machines are sought and these are modified for specialized tasks simply by adapting them to the required production rate. This way of proceeding is the result of the following set of observations:

(1) a written-off machine then has a negligible cost;

(2) the immobilization of an operator costs three to five times more than that of a machine,

(3) the aim is to reduce costs and not to optimize the use of machines.

4.4 THE KANBAN SYSTEM

In order to avoid a shortage of parts in a production process, each workstation must fetch the components it needs from the preceding station according to a manufacturing or assembly programme.

We thus arrive at the idea of the 'reconstitution of consumption' in which each workstation n is a consumer for the upstream $(n-1)$th station and is a producer for the downstream $(n+1)$th station (Fig. 4.6). When a part is taken from a station, a card which accompanies the part is left in place. Although formerly in metal, the card is now no more than a piece of paper containing indications such as the reference number of the product, the quantity, the required date of manufacture.

The card is a document attached to the part or the container, serving as a label for it. This has given the method its name: *Kanban* is Japanese for 'card' or 'sign'.

The Kanban system was developed around 1963 at the same time as the methods for supplying supermarkets, which involved ordering the necessary products only just before they were consumed. The Toyota company who launched the system then reduced intermediate stocks of parts and later did away with them. From 1965, the method was increasingly applied to parts supplied by outside contractors. It took more than 10 years to extend the application of the method to suppliers, something which had not been part of the original concept.

Contrary to a false but quite widespread Western view of Japanese production methods, the Kanban system is mainly a tool used to regulate manufacturing plants and is not something to shackle subcontractors.

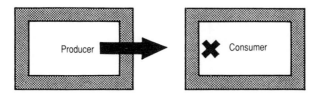

Fig. 4.6.
Part of the Kanban system in which successive workstations are regarded as each others' producer and consumer.

4.4.1   General principles

A Kanban loop generally corresponds to one manufacturing level, i.e. one which is formalized by a level in the bill of materials. The example shown in Fig. 4.7 illustrates the simplest loop, that of the production of a component for a single customer. In practice, the manufacture of a product often involves handling several components, but the principle to be described is easily generalized to a Kanban loop for each link in the bill of materials.

We shall make the assumption that the system upstream which is not shown (another Kanban loop, MRP or stock) always maintains a level of the A components sufficient for the level of the $(N-1)$th production station.

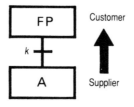

Fig. 4.7.
The simplest type of Kanban loop: the manufacture of a single finished product FP from a single component A via the production process k for a single customer.

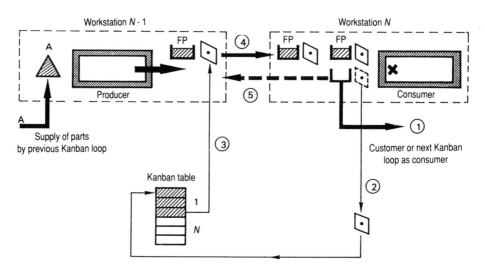

Fig. 4.8.
Generalization of Fig. 4.7: the Nth Kanban loop corresponding to the Nth level in the bill of materials.

In Fig. 4.8, suppose at ① that a customer (or downstream station $N+1$) debits the 'stock' of the product FP by one batch (the batch may be the unit product, a container or a pallet). The card freed in this way returns to the Kanban table of the $(N-1)$th station ②. In the case of containers, the empty container returns to the producer station $N-1$ ⑤. As long as there are cards on the table, the producer takes the oldest of these cards ③, produces the batch of the product FP corresponding to it, attaches the card to this batch and makes sure it arrives at the consumer ④.

4.4.2 Determining the size of Kanban tables

One of the important criteria for the success of a Kanban system is the optimization (minimizing) of the number of cards, i.e. of batches, containers or pallets, in circulation between the producer and the consumer.

If this number is too small, there is a danger of stock failure. If it is too large, the level of intermediate stocks is increased and this makes the method less attractive.

The number of cards in circulation, and hence the size of the table relating to the loop, must be adjusted in terms of the growth in consumption of the product controlled by a Kanban loop (Fig. 4.9). The size N of the table is given by

$$N = \text{batch} + RT + SS,$$

where batch = minimum quantity taken away by the carrier (minimum = one pallet, one part, one container), RT = response time of the loop (or more precisely the buffer absorbing the response time) = (transfer time ④

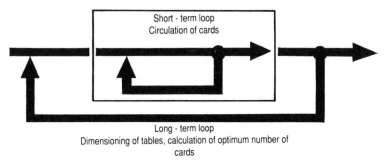

Short - term loop
Circulation of cards

Long - term loop
Dimensioning of tables, calculation of optimum number of cards

Fig. 4.9.
The size of the Kanban table needs to be adjusted as the level of consumption develops.

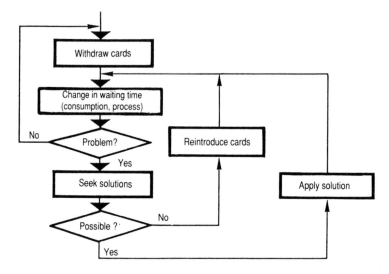

Fig. 4.10.
Optimizing the size of Kanban tables can stimulate a re-examination of the production process and improve it.

+ production time for one batch) × mean consumption (no. of batches/day), SS = safety stock.

The process of optimizing the size of the tables should also stimulate a continual reexamination of the production process (fig. 4.10) and bring improvements to it.

4.4.3   Limitations: coexistence of MRP and Kanban

Kanban triggers production on the basis of past consumption (historic basis). This implies a regular and known consumption, otherwise there would be a need to set up or increase safety stocks and this would make the method less attractive.

Such a procedure is therefore only applicable to repetitive mass production. It will be ruled out when handling individual articles or in a make-to-order context, i.e. with products whose demand is unpredictable (Fig. 4.11(b)).

When some sub-assemblies of individualized products can be manufactured by a standard mass production line method, it becomes a matter of ensuring good coordination between an MRP system (handling of specific orders for marketed products) and a Kanban system (handling the mass production of sub-assemblies with a given regular rate of consumption).

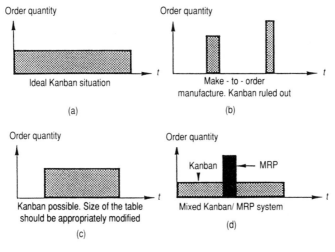

Fig. 4.11.
Limitations of the Kanban method.

Thus, when external orders expand and are taken into account by the calculation of the MRP requirements, the sizes of the Kanban tables must then be automatically readjusted (Fig. 4.11(d)).

4.4.4   Application of the Kanban principle to logistics equipment

In modern integrated production units, the handling of Kanban loops is completely incorporated in the devices used to control logistics activities. Thus, the theoretical method of circulating paper cards is replaced by an exchange of electromechanical signals.

However, the method still involves technology that is very simple, sometimes even quite rudimentary. As an example, we imagine an assembly line in which the supply of components (A and B), manufactured upstream, is controlled by Kanban loops (Fig. 4.12).

Consider the assembly station N in the chain. When a pallet passes in front of it ① with the aim of assembling A and B, the operator helps himself to components on a first-in-first-out (FIFO) gravity feed device (e.g. an inclined channel). Taking a part A actuates a position sensor ② producing an increment on a counter and illuminating one more indicator lamp (or alters a digital display system) on the Kanban table ③ of the producer of A. The same applies to B. The producer of the components will supply the consumer as long as the table is not empty ④. Reception of a new component (or batch components) in the FIFO stock of the consumer will actuate another position sensor ⑤, this time producing a decrement on the counter of the Kanban table, which will have the effect of switching off an indicator lamp (or decrementing the digital display system).

Where there is a common system for controlling the A and B components required as the pallet appears, a memory system attached to each pallet and read during its passage in front of the assembly station actuates an indicator lamp above each compartment of selected components. Such a system is technically very user-friendly and has been installed by the Japanese company, Daikin, on its refrigerator assembly lines.

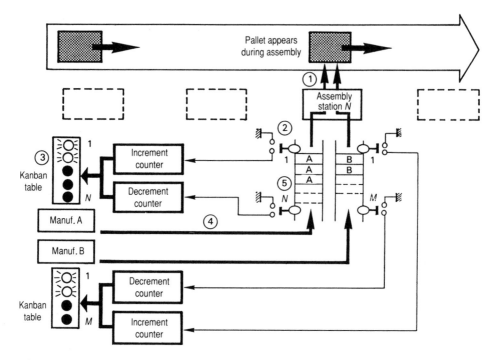

Fig. 4.12.
Application of the Kanban system to the movement and supply of components for a production process.

In the Bull integrated production unit at Villeneuve d'Asq in northern France, the Kanban system has been installed in such a way that the whole supply of components upstream of the assembly stations is carried out automatically. Here, the Kanban tables have been replaced by a system of computers and PLCs which control the wire-guided trucks and other AGVs (automated guided vehicles) of the automated warehouse.

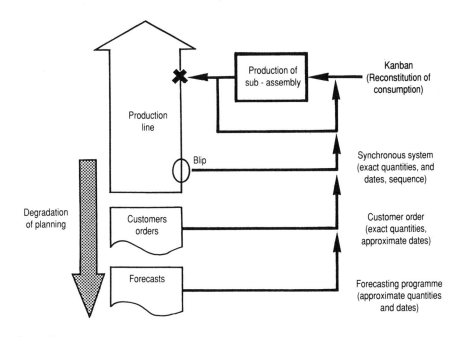

Fig. 4.13.
The synchronous system of production control.

4.5   FROM THE KANBAN SYSTEM TO THE SYNCHRONOUS SYSTEM

When we are able to ascertain the rate of production at any instant and know that it is the same along the whole line, it may be an attractive idea to anticipate the manufacture of components very accurately so that they arrive at the assembly station exactly when they are to be used.

In the Kanban method, the exact time of the next consumption is not known beforehand, so a batch of components is made permanently available while awaiting the next consumption order. This immobilizes in-process components or stock, although in extremely small quantities compared with conventional control systems.

The *synchronous system* (Fig. 4.13) overcomes even this degree of immobilization. However, it does introduce a synchronization blip into the production line upstream of the station ordering the component in question. The position of this synchronization point along the chain is fixed in such a way that the time taken for a pallet to pass from this point to the assembly station is equal to the time needed to make components available at the same station.

5 Structure of Data and Databases

5.1 CIM AND THE STRUCTURE OF MANAGEMENT INFORMATION SYSTEMS

CIM can be viewed as an integrated set of information systems or a *unified information system* enabling every person in the company, at whatever level, to benefit from real-time direct access to all the data needed for their work (Fig. 5.1).

The handling and processing of such data using the resources of information technology requires that they be grouped into files, a structure which facilitates access and allows us to deal with a wide variety of types of information originating from different sources. As a result, it is impossible to provide a reasonable description of the CIM concept without tackling aspects of the structure of data and, more precisely, the concepts of data files and databases. Of course, the approach adopted below will not be that of the specialist in information technology, but is more of an architect's view of an integrated production system.

5.2 FROM FILE-HANDLING SYSTEMS TO DATABASE MANAGEMENT SYSTEMS

The files of data held by most firms are continually evolving, with changes in some having inevitable effects on others. The structure of file-handling systems must therefore be adapted to data-processing methods and must be served by utility programs for the creation, updating, interrogation, deletion, copying, etc. of files. Security and protection are also aspects that have to be taken into account by the system.

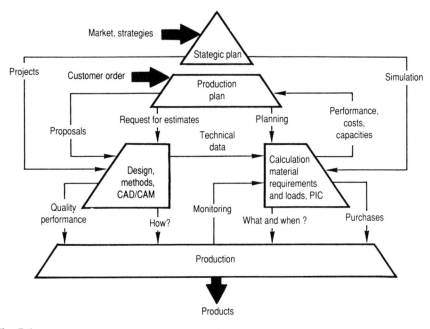

Fig. 5.1.
The production control system.

The classical concept of a file

A file is a collection of homogeneous entities known as *records*. Each record consists of a certain number of headings or *fields*, such as an identification number, a description, a quantity in stock and so on. The most important of these is the *record number, access code* or *key*. which enables this record to be identified among all the others in the file. While a record sometimes has several access codes, it is in most cases unique: the key is in fact a privileged field which serves as an identifier during selective or indexed access to a record without scanning through all the data in the file (Fig. 5.2).

Each field or heading contains one or more characters. As part of a CIM information system, a field may also contain a plan, a view, a digitized image, etc. We shall deal with such generalizations of the idea of a field when we describe multi-media databases in Sec. 5.3.3.

The organization of a file depends on its anticipated use and it will be so structured as to make it easy to handle. File structures fall into one of the following basic categories:

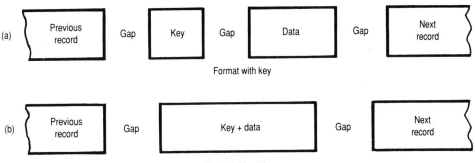

Fig. 5.2.
Examples of possible formats for a record stored on a disc: (a) keyed; (b) 'keyless'. In the latter case, the key is considered as one of the data fields and is essential for the location of the record in the file.

Sequential files, in which the data are classified in the increasing or decreasing values of their keys, enabling a useful record to be found by scanning through the file.

Indexed sequential files, in which it is sufficient to indicate the position of the required record by an index. The sequential nature of the indices means that the data are classified by their access code or key.

Direct access files are intended for applications which always deal with records in a random order. It is not worth classifying these: the search is carried out using the correspondence between the key and the physical address of the record.

Inverted files, of interest when several keys are required to identify a record.

Towards a more global approach

With the classical types of file organization listed above, a given file is optimized for a given application. The database approach is quite different since any file may be accessed through many applications programs. In fact, each individual application may be considered as a channel through which it is possible to search for, or add to, the data in the database.

The database itself can consist of one or many files, the essential idea being that it must be possible to access them in different ways during different applications. For example, it may happen that a file on staff wages, to which access is normally obtained by a key or payroll number, is to be used at the production control level to plan operations in terms of the skills possessed by employees.

The program accessing the database may be a standard program (e.g. calculation of material requirements, management statistics) or so specific that it will be used only once, particularly if large interrogation facilities are available.

It is therefore unwise to attempt to optimize a database for a specific application since, when this has been done, other tasks might very well be less efficiently performed.

5.3 DATABASES AND DATABASE MANAGEMENT SYSTEMS

The database concept depends on the principle that each item of data (in the logical sense and not necessarily in the physical sense) exists only once in the information system but may be accessible to any application. This *non-redundancy* or *uniqueness* enables the integrity of the data to be guaranteed no matter what type of use is made of it.

If an item of data is to be accessed logically by two different applications, its membership of each of the data sets needed for both treatments must be specified (Fig. 5.3).

The implementation of such a system is dominated by two main trends in database design:

(1) Data belonging to the same set are linked to each other by a pointer mechanism. The database is then said to be *navigational* since, to access

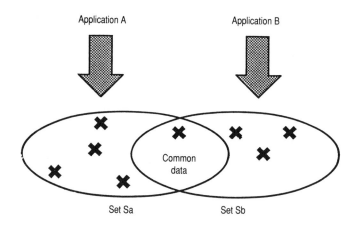

Fig. 5.3.
Items of data (x) accessed by two different application programs need to have their membership of the relevant data sets specified.

data, one moves around with the pointers in the set of data in question, and possibly in subsets of them.

(2) Data are presented in tabular form (relations). A table contains one or more columns identified by a name and corresponding to each of the constituents of the relation. We then speak of a *relational* model. The data structures are very simple and the way they are accessed is never mentioned, unlike navigational databases in which the links predetermine what access is possible.

The concept of logical data independence

A basic aim of data structures is to ensure the durability of information irrespective of the particular choice of hardware made. The database concept introduces an additional layer in the structure called *logical data organization*, which allows records to be manipulated independently of the equipment used for the physical storage of the data.

The input–output operations in an application program are special instructions which work on the *logical database*. The database management system (DBMS) then transforms them into physical input–output operations (Fig. 5.4).

This approach preserves the mutual independence of applications and the ancillary storage devices so that one of them can theoretically be replaced without having any effect on the other.

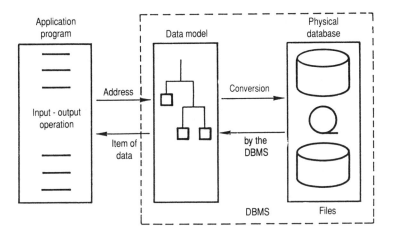

Fig. 5.4.
The database management system is an interface between the logical database and the physical database.

5.3.1   Navigational databases and the CODASYL model

A navigational type of database is a standardized set of data, retrieved and recorded once, linked to each other by a system of pointers enabling useful information to be supplied to different applications.

There are two basic models for navigational databases:

(1) *The hierarchical model*, the basis of the first DBMSs, which should be mentioned for historical reasons;

(2) *The network model*, which is now more widely used.

In the hierarchical model (e.g. the IMS system of IBM and IDS1 of Bull), the fields and records of the data are linked by parent–child relationships. A child can only have one parent, and this quickly makes the logical structure of the data very cumbersome (Fig. 5.5).

The network model, on the other hand, allows a child to have several parents (e.g. the IDS2 system of Bull and IDMS of Culliname). The logical structure is then considerably simplified (Fig. 5.6).

The CODASYL (Conference on Data Systems and Languages) model was created at the beginning of the 1960s at the instigation of the US Department of Defense. It proposed to represent the data system by a network structure and supplied programmers with languages for handling data enabling them to navigate as they please inside the often complex structure that they are assumed to be familiar with.

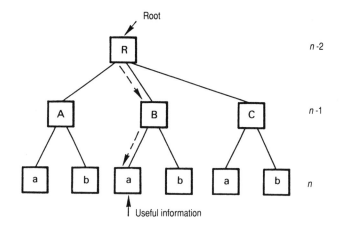

Fig. 5.5.
Hierarchical model for a database. Here R, A, B, a, b are records which may be of different kinds, linked by the relations aA, bA, aB, etc.

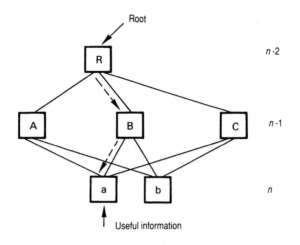

n-2

n-1

n

 Useful information

Fig. 5.6.
Network model for a database. Child records can have several parent records.

Thus, in order to conform to the CODASYL recommendations, a DBMS should consist of the following:

(1) *A network structure for the organization of the data*: this is the heart of the system, formed by the database manager.

(2) *A data description language*, enabling the logical representation of data to be described by a schema and the part exploitable by each application by a subschema.

(3) *A support system description language*, a link between the logical description of the database and the characteristics of the physical units on which it is stored.

(4) *A data manipulation language*, giving the user a means of accessing the database.

The logical structure of CODASYL DBMSs

In order to gain a better appreciation of the advantages and limitations of a network-type DBMS, we shall look a little further into the logical structure of data. The idea of a record, in conventional filing systems (see Sec. 5.2) remains. Thus, a *record* represents an *article, object* or *entity*, and consists of elementary items of data known as *fields* or *headings*. Records representing the same types of object are grouped together to form an entity type.

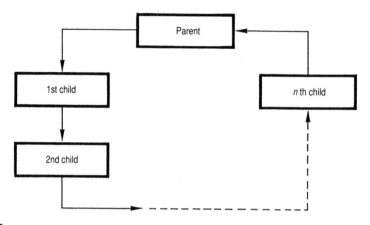

Fig. 5.7.
A closed chain of records in a navigational model, with *next pointers* provided by keys in the various records.

The basic structure of navigational models is the record set. A set consists of (1) one parent record (also called the *owner*), and (2) *n* child records (also called *member* records). Each record is identified by a database key which is unique in the database. The relation between parent and child of a set is embodied in a closed chain. The starting-point of the chain is the parent, which provides the key of the first child and this in turn provides the key of the second child and so on, the last child supplying the key of the parent. We say that each record points to the following one, so that it contains what is called a *next pointer* (Fig. 5.7).

To reduce processing time, backward links are also provided for by the addition of a *prior pointer* on each record of the set. Each child also contains a *direct pointer* to the parent (Fig. 5.8). In the special case of an empty set (no children), the parent points to itself (Fig. 5.9). As an example, we can envisage the parent entity being a customer and the child entities being the orders related to the customer.

If we are now concerned with several customers, then there will be a set of orders for each of them. We then speak of a *set type*, which is a relation between the parent record type (here the customers) and the child record type (here the orders). It then becomes easier to represent the logical structure of the data by graphs showing the set types and the record types called Bachman diagrams (or shorthand representation), rather than by expanded diagrams representing all the records and sets (the longhand representation) (Fig. 5.10).

In the above example, we were looking at a basic set which embodies a $1:N$ (parent:children) relation. This consists of a parent type of entity and

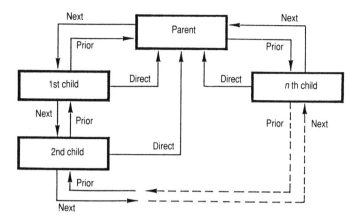

Fig. 5.8.
The chain of Fig. 5.7 with *prior pointers* and *direct pointers*.

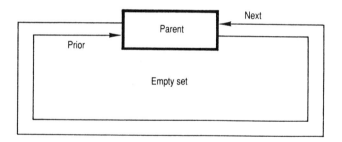

Fig. 5.9.
Empty set.

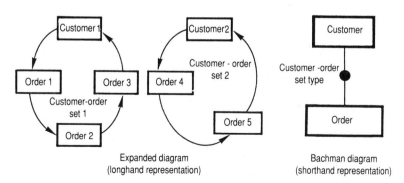

Fig. 5.10.
Illustration of a set type using a Bachman diagram.

a child type of entity (note that the entities of the same type all have the same structure).

In reality, modelling the complete information structure of a company is often reflected in a far more complex representation of the relations between the different types of object being handled. The embodiment of this information system in the form of a database means that we must comply with the structural constraints and hence avoid any form of ambiguity in the subsequent interpretation of the data model. Thus, the various types of set structure encountered in practice are obtained by forming composite structures from basic sets, which guarantee the unique character of the relations between objects.

Any real information system may be modelled using eight fundamental set structures:

(1) the basic set;

(2) the hierarchical structure;

(3) the tree structure;

(4) the multi-type structure;

(5) the simple network structure ($m:n$ relation);

(6) the complex network structure (bills of materials);

(7) the cyclic structure;

(8) the complex structure.

The same type of entity can be the parent in one set and the child in the other. We then speak of *hierarchical structure* (Fig. 5.11). A given set may include several types of article and we shall then say that we have a *multi-type set*. An example is a customer with orders and invoices (Fig. 5.12).

The same type of record can be parent of several sets: this is the *tree-structure* set. Using the same example as before, instead of providing for a multi-type set grouping orders and invoices, it is possible to provide for a customer-order (CO) set and a customer invoice (CI) set (Fig. 5.13).

Up to this point, the various structures considered are equally applicable to a network or a hierarchical model. We now look at a very common case which is a good illustration of the weaknesses of hierarchical databases.

Suppose that the company has to handle a certain number of items in a certain number of warehouses. In the most general (and most common) case, we can imagine that one warehouse contains several types of item just as an item may occur in several warehouses (assumption of distributed stock).

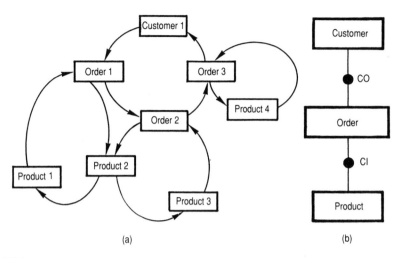

(a)

(b)

Fig. 5.11.
Hierarchical structure: (a) in full; (b) Bachman diagram; CO = customer-order set, CI = customer-invoice set.

The strict parent–child or hierarchical model cannot represent such a structure without duplicating the items for each warehouse that contains it. This redundancy can be avoided with a network model since the same record may belong to several sets. For that reason, we shall say that this involves a *simple network set structure*.

Thus, $m:n$ type relations between entities (here m warehouses for n items) are easily embodied logically in the creation of a 'relationship' or

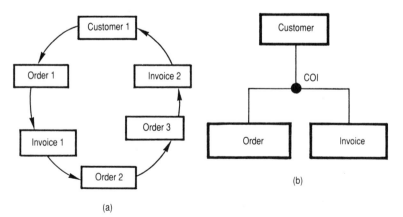

(b)

(a)

Fig. 5.12.
Multi-type set: (a) in full; (b) Bachman diagram.

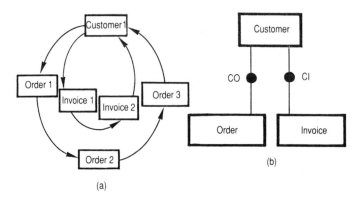

(a)

(b)

Fig. 5.13.
Tree set: (a) in full; (b) Bachman diagram.

'link' entity (here each item 'is stored in' a warehouse), each of these relationship entities being children of entities to be put into correspondence (Fig. 5.14).

A special case of this network structure is the *bill of materials structure* or the *complex network structure*. Here the type of relation becomes unique to a given type of entity. This is because a given item is composed of one or more other items and may also be the component of an item at a higher level. The bill of materials structure plays a fundamental part in the CIM information system (see Sec. 3.2) (Fig. 5.15).

The information structure in a company depends upon the employee-unit flow charts and, of course, handles them. This approach is expressed in the form of a *cyclic set* (Fig. 5.16). A unit-employee set contains all the employees (children) of a unit (parent). An employee-unit set is empty for an employee not occupying a hierarchical station. For a hierarchical superior (parent), it contains one unit (child). There is at least one employee who depends on no superior and thus does not enter into a unit-

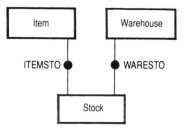

Fig. 5.14.
Set types for $m:n$ relations through the use of a link or relationship as an entity.

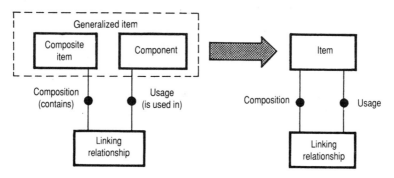

Fig. 5.15.
Bill of materials structure.

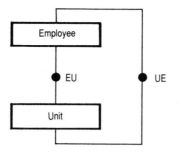

Fig. 5.16.
A cyclic set.

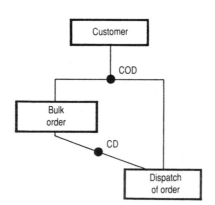

Fig. 5.17.
A complex set.

employee set. The CODASYL model, under certain conditions, accepts the existence of records not attached to a parent.

Finally, a more unusual structure is that known as the *complex set*, which allows access at several levels to certain child entities (Fig. 5.17).

All combinations of the above structures are possible, almost without limit, and this makes it possible to build a faithful model of the real company (see Sec. 6.2.2).

The physical structure of navigational DBMSs

This description of navigational databases and more especially of network systems, brief as it is, would not be complete without considering the physical storage of records and the link between the physical structure of the database and the logical structure of the data. The database consists of a set of files in the classical meaning of the term. The record pointers are stored with user data in the recordings of these files. Figure 5.18 illustrates the simple case of a child record with a single parent.

In practice, as we saw in a network model, a child record may have several parents. In this case, this child record will belong to as many sets as there are direct parents and will have three pointers (next, prior, parent) for each of the sets. In the same way, a parent record may have several children and will thus contain a next pointer and a prior pointer for each set of which it is the parent.

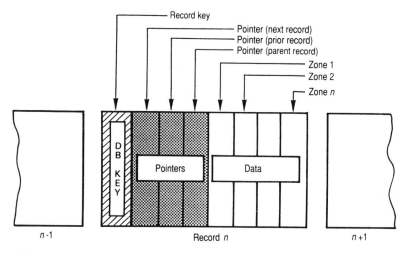

Fig. 5.18.
Physical structure of a child record with a single parent record.

For modular reasons (adaptation to the types of disc used) and thus for reasons of performance, databases are generally organized in areas and pages. All pages have an area of the same size (a multiple of the disc sector). The page contains, apart from a heading and a table of internal physical pointers, the records identified by a line number in the page. It is the page and line numbers which together determine the database key. Data can be accessed using the fundamental instruction of the data manipulation language: *selection*, which allows access to a record in the central memory.

5.3.2 Relational databases

The relational model was introduced in the 1970s through the proposals of E. F. Codd. Its ambitions, among others, were to handle large databases, possibly distributed physically within a computer network, and to give users who were not specialists in information technology easy access to the data.

To do this, the user has only to reply to the question 'WHAT?' (by giving a simple description of the information he wished to access), the system providing an automatic reply to the question 'HOW IS THIS INFORMATION TO BE ACCESSED?' We then speak of an *assertional query* (saying what is wanted without saying how it is to be accessed) as opposed to *algorithmic programming* (saying what is wanted by expressing the way of obtaining it).

The concept of a relational database is based on a representation of data in the form of tables, which form an essential step for the user who is not an expert in information technology: the tabular structure is very simple and is easily understandable by everybody. Thus, all the information in a relational database is explicitly represented at the logical level in an entirely unique way: in the form of values in tables, each table embodying a relation.

The example shown in Fig. 5.19 illustrates a possible table for a customer. Each table represents a set of data of the same kind (in this case, relating to the entity 'customer') gathered together in the form of a two-dimensional table, which can thus be regarded as a flat file.

If, as we have already mentioned, a table represents a type of entity, i.e. a class of object, each row in the table represents one *object* or *entity*. The columns in the table represent a property or characteristic of one type of object or entity. This is the concept of a field or heading which we have already had occasion to meet in the navigational approach. The term *attribute* is also used to denote a column in a table.

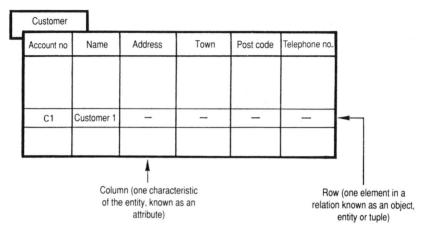

Column (one characteristic
of the entity, known as an
attribute)

Row (one element in a
relation known as an object,
entity or tuple)

Fig. 5.19.
A typical table in a relational database. This is similar to a flat file for a single
customer.

The intersection of a row and column embodies the elementary item of data, i.e. the value of the attribute for a particular occurrence of the type of entity.

Logical structure: tables and set operations

The fundamental characteristic of a relational model is that it is based on *set theory*, which allows us to use relational algebra in manipulating data. In order to gain a better appreciation of this new concept in access to information, we shall use the example shown in Fig. 5.20, which repeats a complex structure already studied in the navigational approach.

Each customer may be concerned with several orders comprising one or more ordered items. The relational concept would logically allow us, for example, to know to whom an order belongs or the orders recorded under a customer. In this case, the relation is embodied in a particular column described as a *foreign key*. This column is an attribute which already exists in another table. The redundancy in the data that it contains then allows the association of (relation between) two (or more) tables.

The property can now be expressed using set theory operations: assume that we are interested in all the orders recorded under the customer whose account number is C1. We only have to carry out the selection operation (SELECT) on the set or the ORDER table to obtain the required solution subset.

The algorithmic approach does not have set theory operations available to it and would have needed a loop program over the set (file) of orders

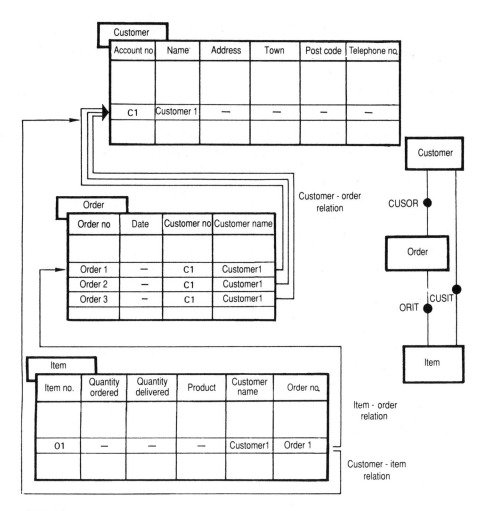

Fig. 5.20.
Example of tables to illustrate the application of set theory ideas in using the logical structure of databases.

in order to extract the solutions:

> for index i from the 1st to the nth record of the order file DO
> > IF customer number attribute of record i = 'C1'
> > THEN display record i
> Next record

The selection operation can work over several attributes and we then speak of multi-criteria queries. In this case we could envisage wanting to extract all the orders of a given customer recorded between two dates $t1$ and $t2$. The query would then be expressed simply, in a language close to natural language:

SELECT from ORDERS where CUSTOMER = C1 and DATE > $t1$ and DATE < $t2$.

This type of query language (e.g. SQL, DBASE3) claiming to be accessible to the user who is not an expert in information technology is called a *fourth-generation language* (4GL), as opposed to third-generation languages (e.g. COBOL, FORTRAN) requiring, as we illustrated above, an algorithmic method of programming which is therefore addressed mainly to information technologists.

In order to bring out clearly the range of possibilities of this new generation of languages, we rely on a particularly powerful fundamental operation in relational algebra: JOIN. This operation makes it possible to extract the most complex information involving several tables in direct or indirect relationships with each other. It depends on the SELECT operation already described and on another operation from set theory: the CARTESIAN PRODUCT.

A Cartesian product is the combination of all the rows in a table with all the other rows in other tables, even if there is no real correspondence (Fig. 5.21).

However, it should be pointed out that the Cartesian product considered here does not have as strict a meaning as the same operation in the mathematical sense. For, if we consider two sets (tables) **A** and **B** such that

$$A = \{x\} \text{ (where } x \text{ is an element (row) of set } \mathbf{A}),$$
$$B = \{y\} \text{ (where } y \text{ is an element (row) of set } \mathbf{B}),$$

then the Cartesian product **A** × **B** in the mathematical sense is the set of pairs (x, y) for any x and y belonging to **A** and **B** respectively. We then have

$$\mathbf{A} \times \mathbf{B} = \{(x, y)\} \neq \mathbf{B} \times \mathbf{A} = \{(y, x)\}.$$

This non-commutation does not persist in the relational algebra of databases, where the elementary pair (x, y) is considered as identical to the pair (y, x). Hence:

$$\mathbf{A} \times \mathbf{B} = \mathbf{B} \times \mathbf{A} \text{ for data.}$$

It is now possible to understand the idea of using JOIN for carrying out selection operations involving several tables. The operation consists in first producing a Cartesian product of all the tables concerned in the query, and

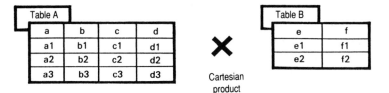

Fig. 5.21.
Illustrating the Cartesian product of two tables.

then carrying out a selection of the rows corresponding to the desired criterion from the Cartesian product table.

Thus, taking as an example the above data model (customer–order–item), imagine that, in order to make efficient use of transport, we wish to know the set of orders (taking all customers together) intended for the same destination (*town* attribute of the customer table) and lying within a range of dates $t1$ to $t2$ (*date* attribute of the order table). The first step in JOIN involves creating the Cartesian product of all the tables whose attributes (columns) occur in the expression giving the final result (town and date of order, hence the Cartesian product of the customer table and the order table).

The selection according to the stated criterion (here the given town and range of dates) is carried out in a second stage on the table resulting from the Cartesian product (customer × order). This selection must also carry a criterion which although implicit in natural language, must nevertheless be spelt out in order to remove any logical ambiguity: this is the expression of the correspondence between the customer references (the order number in the order table must correspond to the account number of the customer table for any given selected row in the Cartesian product). The expression of this latter criterion is called the join equation since it ensures the logical relationship between several tables.

Note that these two steps, which together form the join operation, are expressed in a single query which can be stated as

SELECT from ORDER × CUSTOMER
  where TOWN (CUSTOMER table) = 'PARIS'
    and DATE (ORDER table) > $t1$ and DATE (ORDER table) < $t2$
    and CUSTOMER-NUMBER (ORDER table) = ACCOUNT-NUMBER
    (CUSTOMER table)

Other fundamental relational operators

INTERSECTION, applying only to *tables of the same structure*, extracts all
the rows and retains the *rows common* to two (or more) tables, any
duplication being removed, of course. This is the INTERSECTION operation in the mathematical logic sense.

UNION combines all the rows from *tables of the same structure*, removing
any duplicated rows from the new set (the UNION operation in the
mathematical logic sense).

DIFFERENCE, applying only to *tables of the same structure*, retains only
those rows belonging solely to the first table (i.e. the 'intersection' rows
are excluded).

DIVISION, used very rarely but included for completeness, can be used
if two tables each have a column with the same domain, the 'common'
column. Division is best illustrated by an example in which a binary (two-
column) relation is divided by a unary relation. The division operation
extracts the uncommon column and selects the attributes whose associated
entries in the common column contain all the values of the unary relation.

PROJECTION, like SELECTION, is an *operator acting on a single table* and
enables us to extract one or more named columns from the table.

Physical organization of a relational DBMS

The idea of a relational database can, from a conceptual point of view, be
understood as a tabular structure of information for which there exists a
rigorous method (mathematical set theory) of accessing data. This access
takes the form of queries in a very high level language close to a natural
language.

The underlying physical structure of a relational DBMS follows the
standard organization in indexed sequential files (see Sec. 5.2) which forms
the core of the system. The novel and attractive feature lies in the query
(4GL) layer, which makes the structures *access-transparent* as far as users
are concerned (Fig. 5.22).

Moreover, the programs no longer depend on the access paths. As a
result, unlike CODASYL databases, the relational model does not have
independent languages available for the prior description of the data

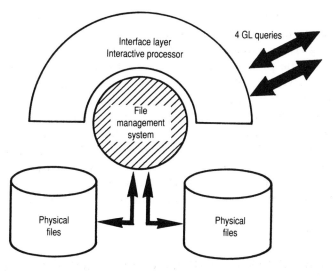

Fig. 5.22.
Queries made in a fourth-generation language are an added layer in relational databases.

model, this being described and managed in interactive form by the same query language that allows access to the information. Thus, in an ORACLE or INFORMIX database system for example, tables are created under the query language SQL. Such a creation or manipulation of tables can even be carried out while the database is being used (selection of data).

It can easily be appreciated that the price to pay for the user-friendliness of fourth-generation languages will be a reduction in the performance of the system. When a system is interrogated by a large number of users with queries that are time-consuming and poorly optimized, or when the data model is created and subsequently modified without great care, response times will undoubtedly become unacceptable.

To obtain a better idea of the processing power required by some users, it is sufficient to appreciate that most of the commonly used queries involve forming the Cartesian product over several tables. Such an operation will create a temporary table often needing a substantial memory capacity, and will then perform the selection process by scanning through this substantial set for the required data. As an example, the Cartesian product of two tables with reasonable dimensions of 100 rows and 10 columns will end up with a table having 10 000 rows and 20 columns!

As a result, the relational approach has not replaced navigational databases and third-generation languages. Thus, CODASYL has remained synonymous with high performance (rapidity of access), with automatic control over the integrity of data (security) and with shared access (many users), making it a system particularly well suited to remote transaction processing. The rapid access to information through repetitive transactions will remain the preferred domain of third-generation language programs used with navigational data structures. The main advantages of relational databases and 4GL query languages are the flexibility of access and the ease with which data structures are created and then manipulated.

The real world, however, is not compartmentalized and is constantly evolving, so that it is now possible to access CODASYL databases using 4GL-type query languages (e.g. the IQS system of Bull), and there are many efforts currently being made whose aim, in the medium term, is to allow the efficient use of relational databases in remote transaction processing.

5.3.3   The CODASYL–relational dilemma in the choice of a CIM information structure

A CIM information structure, which has to carry the flow of all the data to any location in the system, can now be chosen from one of the following two models.

(1)   A data structure based on a central source (Fig. 5.23)

This is still the most widely used model today. Built on a CODASYL-type DBMS, this structure provides complete integrity of the data and an excellent performance to a large number of users connected simultaneously. The other side of the coin, as we have already seen, is the need to predefine for the user the set of access paths to the data and the need to have available a closed set of transactions. These transactions or programs are developed in a third-generation language (because of its high performance) from algorithms that are sometimes complex and hence remain the prerogative of specialists in information technology.

This is the preferred area of *applications packages* such as computer-integrated production control, which are developed by specialist service companies and some of the designers in information technology. These offer ready-made solutions suitable for many specifications as long as the main constraints stay close to a standard.

The 'applications package' approach is to be recommended to any company in which the production conditions conform to a standard classical model, in which the information structure is relatively stable over a period of time and in which there is a desire to be free from the need to

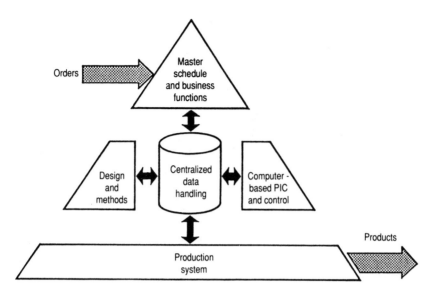

Fig. 5.23.
A data structure based on a central source.

keep the application continually up to date (applications software being particularly prone to the launching of new versions and to the issuing of lists of corrections to previous versions).

Moreover, this type of method offers a 'guided' procedure for its implementation. Users do not necessarily need to define the concepts and the methods of applying them, but can simply be content with finding things out for themselves in a kind of apprenticeship with the product. The implementation of such methods fits perfectly into the framework of a management schema and more particularly into an approach of the top-down type, i.e. starting from the most general level of the company and proceeding towards the most specific level, that of the machines in the workshops. Note that the applications package type of solution, whose main feature is a high degree of standardization, does not concern itself very much with the integration of the process or workshop functions specific to each unit.

(2)   A data-sharing structure organized by a central control system (Fig. 5.24)

Theoretically, this is the model for the future. Its structure is based on the principle of a distributed relational database, whose only drawbacks at present are its performance when a large number of users are connected

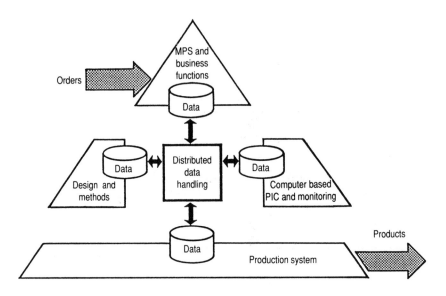

Fig. 5.24.
A data-sharing structure organized by a central control system.

simultaneously to the same server, and a control over the integrity and security of data that is not yet as thorough as that of CODASYL systems. Although these weaknesses make them systems which are still very often (and sometimes even too often) limited to laboratory applications, the versatility and virtues of the concept have already become legendary.

Market fluctuations and their effects on the production process or, more generally, on entire companies, lead to an almost perpetual re-examination of their information systems. The continual restructuring is intensified still more by the increasing availability of new NC technology. However, the model we are now discussing depends on a relational database, so that the system can easily be made-to-measure, and later adaptations of it can in practice be devised by the users (initiates) themselves while it is still running.

Moreover, very few industrialists are willing to follow a new path without there being a possible fall-back position should the outcome prove to be unsatisfactory. The voice of wisdom also counsels them to tackle any large-scale project through a highly coordinated succession of sub-projects whose consequences can be better monitored and on which it is easier to concentrate the energy of the company. Note that this approach can be generalized to any physical or economic process which is more easily reversible if carried out without serious disruptions. These are the elementary principles which form the basis of any master plan in organization.

We can see that the implementation of a CIM system necessarily involves several projects when we realize that each of them often requires dedicated hardware. Thus, although the development needs to be carried out in the context of a global approach, its component parts will be physically installed in a modular form as it progresses.

A basic feature of relational DBMSs is that they can be used in a distributed environment, so that these data-sharing structures are a perfect response to the constraints of modularity imposed by a CIM approach.

Each project (CAD application, handling of technical data, the production plan, MRP, process supervision) will be resident in a specific server with its own local database. This server will, of course, have access to common data stored in other servers, through a local area network (see Sec. 2.6). The uniqueness and integrity of the global data structure is ensured through the local network by a central database management system (e.g. SQL–NET on ORACLE, INGRES–NET on INGRES).

The global development of a distributed information system will be achieved through a data distribution procedure, whose aim is to propose rules specifying the places where the data and the data processing are resident. These rules can be briefly summarized as follows:

(1) If the information is used by a single node in the network (server), it will be resident in this server.

(2) If the information is required at several nodes, it will be located at the node which carries out the 'heaviest' processing; other nodes will have access to the data (during transactions or 'light' processing) through the network.

(3) If the information is sought by several nodes at similar frequencies of use, the data will be duplicated physically in each of the servers; periodic (batch) processing to control the integrity of the common data must then be provided for (i.e. simultaneous updating at different places); such processing will use the local area network as the exchange medium. This rule should be treated with caution since it is contrary to the database philosophy.

The principle of data distribution and thus of a functional division of the application may, to a very limited degree, make it possible to circumvent the shortcomings in the performance of relational databases subjected to a large number of simultaneous user connections.

It is sometimes possible to reduce the number of potential users of a server by an additional splitting of its standard functions into sub-applications distributed over several servers. For example, an application program for business management and purchasing supporting up to 20 terminals on the same server could be envisaged as one application distributed over three servers: (1) an application for upstream business management with 10 terminals, (2) an application for control of dispatches with 5 terminals and (3) purchasing control with 5 terminals, the functional exchanges between these functions taking place through a local network.

5.3.4   Multi-media databases

The problem

The CIM approach involves the unification of all the information necessary for the company to function. Such information occurs in the most diverse forms, particularly when it concerns technical documentation which may include graphics, plans, pictures, speech, text, etc. Information systems built around classical databases (CODASYL or relational) only take into account data in numeric or alphanumeric form and not that in the form of images, graphics, voices, etc.

The importance of integrating the latter types of data into a single information structure no longer needs to be justified. In most companies, the volume of technical documentation is increasing year by year. Moreover, the complexity of the documents, being related to the sophistication of the products, is also on the increase. If more time has to be devoted to handling the documentation, it will undoubtedly be to the detriment of other tasks of paramount importance, yet to neglect it would be to run the risk of making more mistakes.

A first generation of facilities for dealing with this problem has appeared in recent years, with word processing, CAD/CAM systems, classification systems and document search systems. These bring a local solution to a part of the problem, but they communicate with each other only with difficulty since each has its own way of encoding data. They were designed at a time when the technology available did not allow documents to be stored in databases or to be consulted on the screen because of the space needed in the bulk memory, because of the resultant throughputs over the networks and because of the complexity of the underlying data models.

Although these first-generation facilities provide services that are of even more value today, an increasing number of companies feel the need to change to a second generation which can handle the new type of document (described as multi-media because of the wide range of representations to be dealt with) on an integrated electronic medium. Communication between complementary applications imposes the need to use à standardized code. It then becomes possible, by connecting these facilities through a network, to build an integrated system for the production and use of multi-media technical documentation. Current technical specifications in the field of bulk memory and local networks are such that the contents of these documents can be stored in databases and consulted interactively on high-definition graphic screens.

Main difficulties and possible solutions

The multi-media database approach is faced with two types of difficulty: those related to the volume of data and those related to the complexity of the information to be represented.

The volumes to be handled are very large: a coded A4 page (21 × 29.7 cm^2) occupies a memory space of about 6 kilobytes (kb) for text, 12 kb for graphics and 60 kb for facsimile (compressed).

When speech or images other than fax images are involved, the volumes are even greater: about 160 kb for a black and white TV picture (compressed), about 500 kb for a colour TV picture (compressed) and between 20 and 80 kb for speech lasting one second (depending on the quality).

Thus, in a medium-sized company (about 500 employees), the volume of multi-media technical documentation, even when limited to text, graphics and facsimile, generally amounts to tens or hundreds of gigabytes (10^9 bytes) and in some cases terabytes (10^{12} bytes).

If all the employees consult this documentation on screen several hours per day, the throughput in the network will amount to several megabits per second (10^6 bit/s).

These problems have now been partly solved. Digital optical discs (two gigabytes for a 30 cm diameter double-sided disc) seem to be a suitable support medium, although still too slow. 'Jukeboxes' of 100 double-sided digital optical discs are being developed, but the disc-changing problem (about 10 seconds) has not yet been satisfactorily solved. A significant advance has also been made in the network field with the development of networks having a throughput of several megabits per second, possibly twinned with broadband video cable channels.

Moreover, multi-media documents have a structure (logical and physical) that can only be represented using relations between complex objects which themselves have a recurrent and/or complex structure. Such a structure is not very compatible with the limitations in the DBMS data models that are most widely used at present.

Without questioning the value of navigational and relational models (see Secs 5.3.1 and 5.3.2), which are well suited to the representation of digital or alphanumeric data, the description of complex data undoubtedly needed some new concepts and these were developed at the beginning of the 1980s. The new models, embodied in systems still at the prototype stage, were the first to offer the beginnings of a solution to the problems raised by multi-media documents. As examples, we quote the following:

(1) The AGREGATIF (or BIG) model developed by CERFIA of Toulouse, which generalizes the concept of 'information' by using the concept of an 'abstract type' inspired by the ADA language.

(2) The TIGRE model of IMAG in Grenoble, which proposes an extension of the 'Entity–Relationship' model in order to include complex data. This extension is based on the notion of a 'type constructor'.

(3) The ODM (Office Data Model), developed in Toronto, which uses the concepts of objects, object type, generic object type, etc.

(4) The MMD (Model for Multi-media Documents) developed at the Milan Polytechnic Institute and which proposes a syntactic description of data.

(5) The LRDM (Langage de Représentation de Documents Mixtes) which has been developed by INSA (National Institute for Applied Sciences) at Lyon and which proposes a syntactic description of multi-media data based on ODA standardization (Office Document Architecture: CCITT-T-73, ECMA-101 or ISO-8613 standards).

6 Methods for the Analysis and Design of an Information System

6.1 IMPORTANCE OF A METHOD FOR DESIGNING AN INFORMATION SYSTEM

In the various stages leading up to the implementation of a CIM system, the path from the initial expression of the requirements to the development of the application itself generally requires the use of a method for designing and developing the information system. Such a method involves formalizing the requirements laid down in the specifications and expressing them in a *structured model of the real system*. The method should also make it possible:

(1) to organize the running of the overall project by a rational division of tasks, since the whole undertaking is so vast;

(2) to propose a procedure for carrying it out;

(3) to describe or finalize user specifications in an exhaustive manner;

(4) to fix in advance the points at which the progress of the project will be validated and at which decisions will be made.

An effective method should embrace the all three of the ideas illustrated in Fig. 6.1: the life cycle, the methodology and the modelling techniques. It will then be capable of producing standardized data-processing facilities, of ending up with a result that is satisfactory as regards lead time, cost and quality, and of guaranteeing the maintenance and further development of the system.

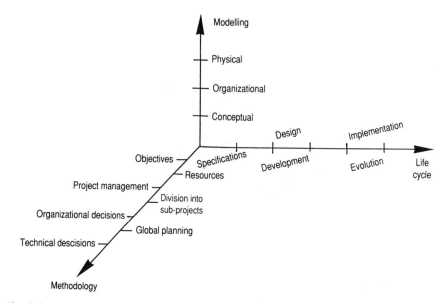

Fig. 6.1.
The three dimensions in the design and development of a product.

The idea of a *life cycle* becomes important when we realize that the life expectancy of an information system is limited to six or seven years, so that we have to envisage looking at its further development some two or three years after it has been implemented.

The fact that the system has such an uncertain future underlines the importance of *methodology*, whose aim is to provide coherence between the information system and its general objectives. The decisions it requires are of two types, one involving the functionalities of the system (e.g. objectives, limitations, organization, technical options), and the second involving the development strategy (e.g. resources to be committed, division into stages, planning).

Finally, *modelling techniques* provide representations of reality that vary with the level of detail or complexity required. A hierarchy of levels will enable us to change the degree of refinement in the model: from an overall general view at the conceptual level to a set of specialized representations for use when physical implementation is involved.

Note that the concept of a 'model' has been intimately associated with science from its very beginnings. The physical laws we have learned to use are nothing more than models or representations of reality. The real system may be represented in different ways depending on the model that is adopted, e.g. the properties of electrons in atoms can be described in terms of waves or particles. Moreover, the physical sciences often set up

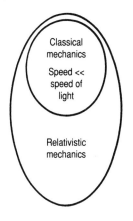

Fig. 6.2.
A hierarchy of physical models. The special theory of relativity developed by Einstein is a more widely applicable and more complex model than classical mechanics, but the latter covers most everyday phenomena.

a hierarchy of models representing the real world, and the model actually used will depend on the field of study in question (Fig. 6.2).

There are several methods now on the market which are aimed at the design and development of information systems: MERISE, Information Engineering, SADT, SD/SA, IDA, AXIAL and so on. We examine two of these in more detail:

MERISE, through its ability to deal with all three dimensions (life cycle, methodology and modelling) and to produce models at several levels, is remarkably well suited to the design and production of CIM applications or of extended computer-based PIC systems. However, the method has not yet penetrated the English-speaking world and still has to accommodate certain technical developments such as support for multi-media data.

SADT (Structured Analysis and Design Technique) is recommended for the analysis of real-time systems, as would be needed for running a manufacturing plant for instance. It is more a method of specification than a tool for the design and production of vast information systems. It leads to an approach of the 'problem-solution' type in which the solution to a problem is deduced from its specifications.

6.2   MERISE—THE GUIDING PRINCIPLES OF THE MODEL

The success of MERISE is largely due to its quite elaborate modelling principle being in complete harmony with the demands of the methodol-

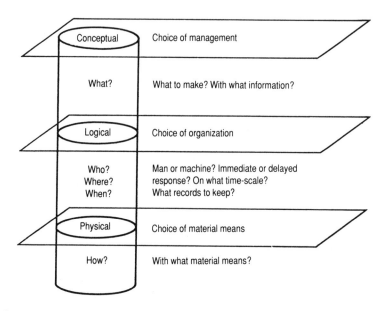

Fig. 6.3.
The three levels of the MERISE method.

ogy employed. These features owe a lot to the links it has with university research on databases and the practical methodology of the large software engineering companies (SSIIs—Sociétés de Service en Ingénierie Informatique) to which the designers belong.

In order to provide an exhaustive description of the data and processes involved in a particular application, it is recommended that the problems to be solved should be split into a hierarchy with several levels. The analytical procedure then evolves from the general to the particular, tackling the whole of a domain before dealing with each of its subsets thoroughly and in detail.

The MERISE method distinguishes three levels: (1) a conceptual representation responding to WHAT; (2) logical models responding to WHO MAKES WHAT and WHERE, thus sharing the data and processing between men and machines as to locations and responsibilities, and (3) the physical level defining the HOW, to provide for the development of the system finally adopted (Fig. 6.3).

The design of the system-to-be is then considered level by level, avoiding the need to go back from an advanced stage of one to a less advanced stage of another, always a costly process. We speak of the 'decreasing degree of invariance' of the levels. Specialist knowledge is required for

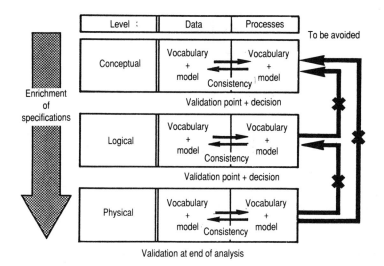

Fig. 6.4.
Designing a system by considering each level in turn.

each of them and this is coordinated through a common vocabulary, formal representations and validation points (Fig. 6.4).

The MERISE method recommends separate analysis of the data and the processes at each level. Care must be taken to check the consistency of both analyses before validation and passing on to the next level.

Organic analysis of the information structure assumes that all the data of the system, their logical relationships and the situations in which they are used, are predetermined. MERISE expresses the results of the functional analysis by means of (1) conceptual models of data and of processes, (2) logical models of data and of processes and (3) physical models of data (forming the data dictionary) and of processes (external and internal).

6.2.1 The conceptual data model

During the implementation of an integrated information system, the sheer size of the project means that all the information to be processed must be dealt with rationally and exhaustively so as to build the database in a succession of ordered and predefined stages, thus avoiding the need for local re-examination or backtracking in the project.

The first, conceptual, stage of the data analysis uses the following procedure:

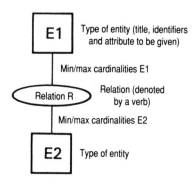

Fig. 6.5.
Entity types associated through a relation.

(1) All the data involved in the project are listed. In the present case of a CIM project, all the departments in the company will be concerned (marketing, research and development, methods, workshops, warehouses, etc). In this way, a complete list of the types of elementary data to be used is drawn up.

(2) These data are grouped into 'packets' identified by a label, i.e. a code having a one-to-one correspondence with the data type and enabling any occurrence of the record or entity to be defined.

(3) A title or name representing a class of objects is allocated to each packet or entity type formed as in (2).

(4) The relations between the entity types are then analysed, i.e. the associations between entity types are specified by a verb. The cardinality of the associations, i.e. how many times (minimum and maximum) the association can occur, is then indicated (Fig. 6.5).

Note that there are four possible types of association at the conceptual level (Fig. 6.6). We can imagine, as an example, that the analysis of the

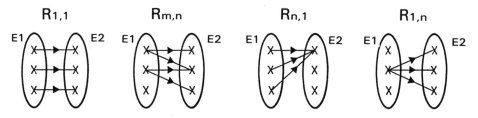

Fig. 6.6.
The four possible types of association at the conceptual level.

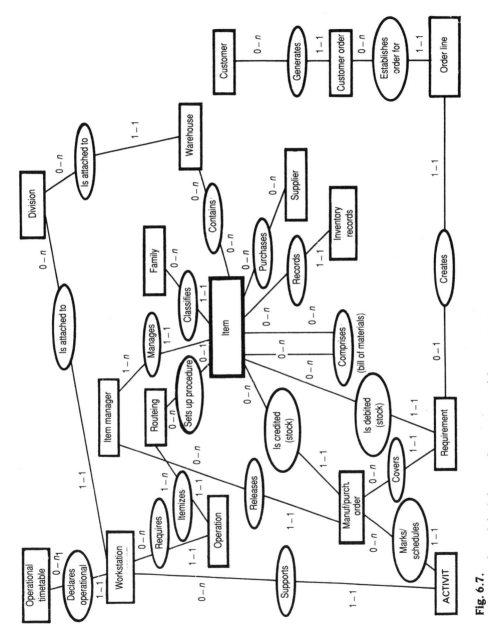

Fig. 6.7.
Conceptual model of the production control function in CIM.

Table 6.1
Typical examples of entities and their attributes to be found in the technical data function of a CIM information system

00 Item	01 Workstation
Attributes	**Attributes**
01 Item reference no—identifier	01 Workstation code—identifier
02 Item designation—(identifier)	02 Workstation designation—
03 Unit of measurement	(identifier)
04 Number of machines	03 Type of station (internal/
05 Type of order (purch./manuf.)	subcontractor)
06 Min. batch (manuf. or purch.)	04 Number of machines
07 Safety stock	05 Number of operators
08 Period for assembly of batch	06 Efficiency of station (%)
09 Fixed completion lead time	07 Accounting charge code—
10 Proportional completion lead time	(identifier)
11 Quantity in stock available	08 Operational timetable
12 Quantity in stock unavailable	09 Nominal daily capacity
13 Quantity in process of manuf.	10 Maximum daily capacity
14 Quantity reserved (or allocated on	11 Hourly machine cost
order	12 Hourly direct labour cost
15 Calculated batch for standard cost	13 Overheads (hourly cost)
16 Standard value-added cost	
(manufactured item)	
17 Standard materials cost	
(manufactured item)	
18 Standard overheads (manufactured	
item)	
19 Standard purchase cost from factory	
(purchased item)	
20 Mean weighted purchase cost	
21 Final purchase cost	
22 Production cost	

function 'technical data' (see Sec. 3.2) of a CIM information system reveals among other things the two entities shown in Table 6.1 with their respective attributes (data types).

After analysing the associations, the conceptual model of the production control function of a CIM project could be expressed by the schema shown in Fig. 6.7.

6.2.2   The logical data model

The aim of the conceptual level is to formalize the specifications of the users and designers of the project clearly and with a common representation. This model then has to be adapted to the functional requirements of the database management systems. Rather than tackle the organic analysis directly, i.e. taking account of the characteristics of the data-processing system used (type of DBMS, languages) at this stage, MERISE proposes an intermediate level of analysis: the logical model. This level restructures the conceptual model into a representation theoretically accessible to any data-processing system by freeing it from being restricted to particular products (e.g. type of computer, physical storage of files) or even to particular types (e.g. relational DBMSs, CODASYL, classical file-handling systems).

The logical data model specifies, among other things, the responsibility for the creation and updating of the variation items of information, their geographical location and the data access points. It also deals with the functional aspects of the communications network.

The importance of this stage is to have a representation of the data and the processes which can easily be carried by any hardware whatsoever. Since data-processing systems become outdated much more quickly than conceptual models, a company will no longer be fettered by the shackles of proprietary systems and will only be dependent on suppliers of systems *in situ*.

Adopting the logical view of data means that the conceptual model must be subjected to two operations as given under the headings below.

(1)   The transformation of any $m:n$ association into a $1:n$ association

In other words, transforming all the relations of the conceptual schema into functions, mappings or bijections. This new representation of the data then allows all the set theory operations possible with the DBMSs to be carried out (see Sec. 5.3).

The elimination of an $m:n$ relation involves replacing it by two functions of the $1:n$ and $1:m$ type as shown in Fig. 6.8.

(2)   The decomposition of some entities into modules

A module is a set of indissociable attributes (always possessed simultaneously), capable of taking as many different values as there are elements in the module (e.g. as many different names or different addresses as there are customers).

The relations between modules are of the same kind as those between entities. Whereas at the overall (conceptual) level, the analysis only involves entities and their relations, the decomposition of each entity containing many elements into modules may allow a considerable optimi-

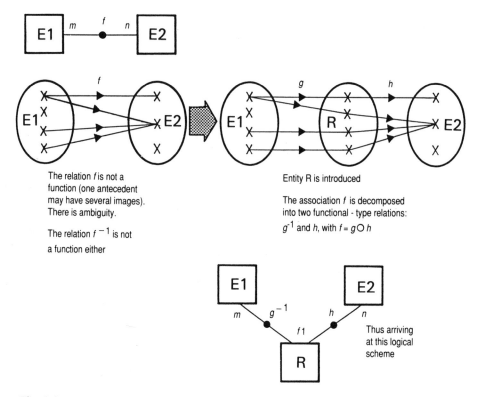

The relation f is not a function (one antecedent may have several images). There is ambiguity.

The relation f^{-1} is not a function either

Entity R is introduced

The association f is decomposed into two functional - type relations: g^{-1} and h, with $f = g \bigcirc h$

Thus arriving at this logical scheme

Fig. 6.8.
Elimination of an $m:n$ relation by replacing it with two functions.

zation of the model to be achieved. During a functional analysis, it is common practice to incorporate some entities in others. In Fig. 6.9(a), for example, the 'operation description' entity is not provided for, but is an attribute incorporated in the 'operation' entity. The 'operation' entity of the conceptual model becomes a set of two modules 'operation' and 'operation description' in the logical data model (Fig.6.9(b)). This approach has the advantage, when an operation does not have an accompanying text (optional attribute), of not encumbering the database with useless attributes. Since the 'operation' entities are reduced to a minimum number of attributes, their processing will be all the more efficient. This method also makes it possible to accept repeated attributes, for example in the event of customers having several possible delivery addresses.

By transforming the conceptual model of the production control function described in Sec. 6.2.1 (Fig. 6.7), we arrive at the logical model shown in Fig. 6.10.

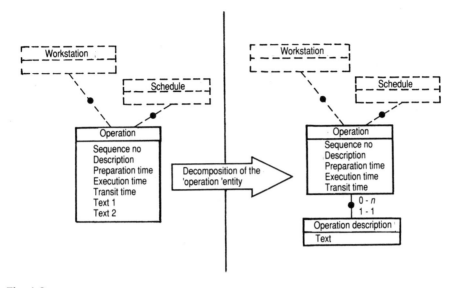

Fig. 6.9.
Example of the decomposition of an entity into modules.

6.2.3   The physical data model and the data dictionary

Given the validated logical model and a fixed hardware and software environment, we begin on the study of the physical data model, an essential preliminary to the strategy of software production and thus to its actual development.

The physical model of the data enables us to specify the layout of data in the machine. Each item of data must be unambiguously located and defined. After making an estimate of the required space, checking the configuration and listing the organizational requirements, the team responsible for carrying out the project undertakes the formation of the data dictionary. This involves a description of each attribute in the form of a data sheet, indicating in general:

(1) a reference number for the files;

(2) a complete designation;

(3) an accurate definition;

(4) a symbolic reference;

(5) a list of possible homonyms or synonyms;

(6) a structure (the kind of features forming the attribute and the length);

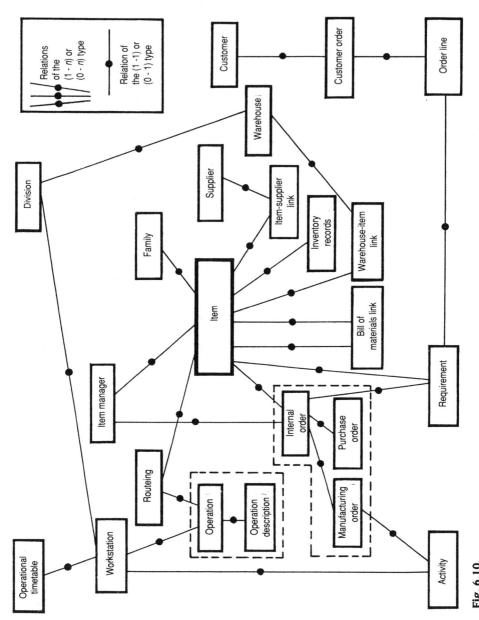

Fig. 6.10.
The logical model of the conceptual model in Fig. 6.7.

(7) possible codification;

(8) the method of obtaining it if it is a question of computed or calculated attributes.

It is only at this stage of the physical data model that the data-accessing techniques are defined (primary keys, secondary keys, inverted lists, pointers). A logical data model can thus be applied equally well to a CODASYL DBMS or a relational system. The physical model will determine the choice of any hardware that is still uncertain.

Since the physical data model is completely integrated into the hardware being used, MERISE does not recommend any special formalism for the representation. Similarly, the standard vocabulary uses the terms 'attribute', 'record', 'segment', 'link', etc. but here the designer's terminology is preferred.

6.2.4 Description of processes

A process is always related to an event. The event is an arrival of information coming from outside the analysed system (e.g. the arrival of a telexed order from a customer or the receipt of components from a supplier). A process can also be the result of a decision (releasing a manufacturing order) or a malfunction (breakdown of a machine). A particular type of event is the arrival of a due date (e.g. H-hour, D-day, end of the week, end of the month) which triggers a process.

All the processes resulting from an event are carried out in the form of one or more transactions in sequence with certain procedures (setting up a machine, manufacturing, followed by a process supervision transaction; preparation of a list of parts to be used, followed by a stock movement transaction and so on).

Analysing processes as part of a CIM project is generally much more complex than applications in classical management. This is because the special feature of information technology when integrated into an industrial environment is that its role is not just that of transforming information into other information but the more difficult one of transforming information into action on objects or materials, i.e. of transforming it into work (in the energy sense of the term) in a totally controlled manner.

A transaction is part of an event processed by the information system at a given instant at a given place. It consists of (1) input of data (through files, terminal keyboards or physical sensors), (2) data processing, (3) output of results (in files, on VDU screens, on paper or to instruments giving readings of physical magnitudes).

The first level in the analysis of processes recommended by MERISE is to start by identifying all the events which the project will take into consideration. The elementary processes will be specified and the conditions for triggering or synchronizing the processes will also be defined at this point.

An example of the descriptive formalism of the MERISE *conceptual* process model is shown in Fig. 6.11, which illustrates the classic scenario of an MRP2 production control system.

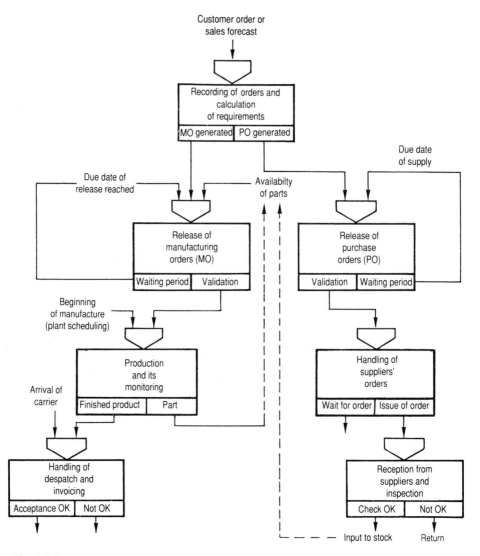

Fig. 6.11.
Conceptual process model for the production control function: MO = manufacturing order; PO = purchase order.

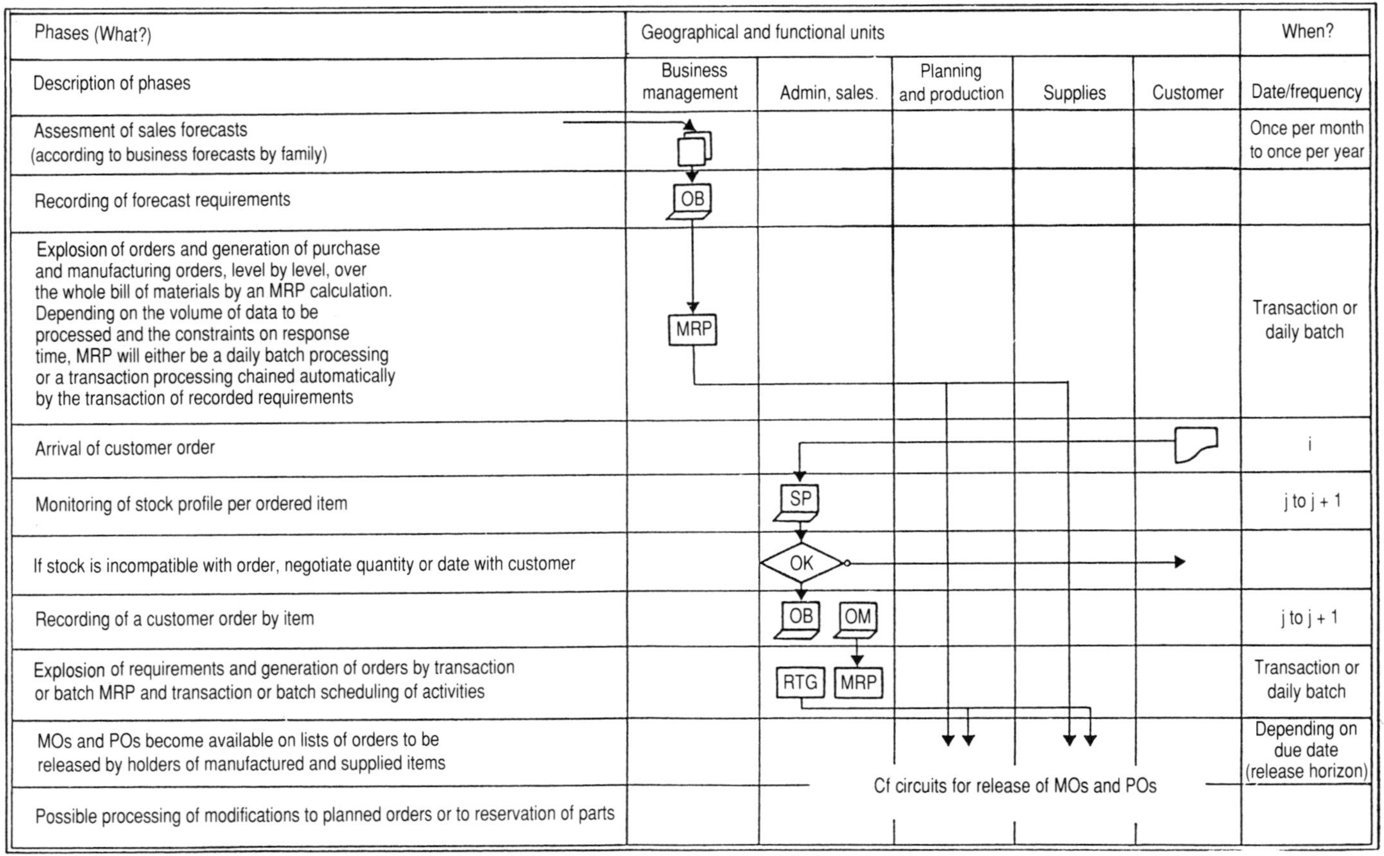

Phases (What?)
Geographical and functional units
When?
Description of phases
Business management
Admin, sales.
Planning and production
Supplies
Customer
Date/frequency
Assesment of sales forecasts (according to business forecasts by family)
Once per month to once per year
Recording of forecast requirements
OB
Explosion of orders and generation of purchase and manufacturing orders, level by level, over the whole bill of materials by an MRP calculation. Depending on the volume of data to be processed and the constraints on response time, MRP will either be a daily batch processing or a transaction processing chained automatically by the transaction of recorded requirements
MRP
Transaction or daily batch
Arrival of customer order
i
Monitoring of stock profile per ordered item
SP
j to j + 1
If stock is incompatible with order, negotiate quantity or date with customer
OK
Recording of a customer order by item
OB
OM
j to j + 1
Explosion of requirements and generation of orders by transaction or batch MRP and transaction or batch scheduling of activities
RTG
MRP
Transaction or daily batch
MOs and POs become available on lists of orders to be released by holders of manufactured and supplied items
Depending on due date (release horizon)
Cf circuits for release of MOs and POs
Possible processing of modifications to planned orders or to reservation of parts

Fig. 6.12.
The logical process model for the job of recording orders and calculation of net requirements: OB = order booking; SP = stock profile; OM = order modification; RTG = routeing.

By making as much headway as this in the analysis, the logical process model and the logical data model between them enable the most detailed possible study to be undertaken without considering the organic aspect, i.e. the characteristics of the hardware environment.

The aim of the *logical* process model is to define (a) the method by which the process should be carried out (man–machine exchanges), (b) the responsibility for carrying it out or for triggering it and (c) its timetable or periodicity. This involves replying to the questions, 'Who makes what at what place and at what time?'

From the conceptual model previously elaborated, the logical or organizational process model is developed for each unit or task identified (see Fig. 6.12).

Finally, the *external physical* process model specifies:

(1) The type and characteristics of the hardware such as the CPU, the discs, the terminals.

(2) The number of machines, VDUs, etc. and their geographical location.

(3) The characteristics of the networks (e.g. medium, throughput).

(4) The VDU and printer models.

The *internal physical* process model will deal with the following:

(1) The running of the processes (e.g. analysis of transactions, interconnection of VDUs, etc.).

(2) The basic software (operating system, communication).

6.3   THE SADT METHOD IN THE FUNCTIONAL ANALYSIS OF MANUFACTURING PLANT AND MANUFACTURING SYSTEMS

The SADT (Structured Analysis and Design Technique) method was developed in the USA by the SofTech Corporation. It was designed to solve the usual problems of specification by starting from requirement analysis. It depends on the following basic concepts:

(1) Any system may be considered as a collection of data.

(2) SADT is used to build a model or a representation of all the functions of a system and their relationships.

(3) A SADT model is a descending, modular, hierarchical and structured representation of reality. Thus, a complex system is analysed step by

step by splitting it into simple structured elements in order to consider the whole model.

The SADT method is based more particularly on a fundamental principle: everything to be analysed must be in no more than six 'boxes' (or modules) in order to ensure that, while a representation gives sufficient detail to make it worthy of interest, it nevertheless remains easy to understand.

The context of a box or module (data module or activity module), i.e. its relationship to other modules, is indicated by arrows (Fig. 6.13), which represent constraints on the links between boxes and not instructions or sequences in the strict sense. The function in the box is only performed when the necessary input from upstream boxes is received through the input arrows. We say that a module is executed when the input arrows are validated. The outputs from a box may be the inputs or controls of other boxes (Fig. 6.14).

Since the SADT procedure involves making a diagram of the problem and not of the information system, this is said to be an approach of the problem-solution type, i.e. the solution to a problem is derived from a description of its specification. Such a method is often not very suitable for building large information systems (e.g. PIC systems integrating the

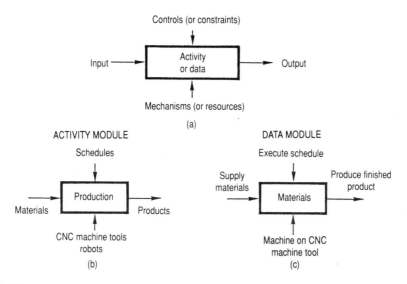

Fig. 6.13.
Boxes or modules representing an activity or data: (a) general form; (b) activity module; (c) data module.

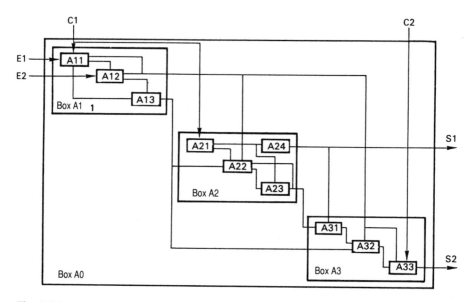

Fig. 6.14.
Method of decomposition in SADT. The box (or function) A0 can be decomposed into three boxes A1, A2, A3; A1 in turn is decomposed into simple elements A11, A12, A13, and so on until the required degree of detail is reached.

functions of purchasing, sales, invoicing, etc.). It is more of a formalized integrated tool of forecasts and requirements than a design method in the proper sense of the term. On the other hand, SADT is a method to be recommended for the analysis of real-time systems at the frontiers of process control, areas in which the effectiveness of simulation techniques is also encountered. In this guise, SADT is at present highly valued in the functional analysis of information systems in work centres and automated production cells.

From the simple statement of the problem expressed formally by box A0 (Fig. 6.15), it is split into as many levels as necessary using other boxes (Figs 6.16 and 6.17). Whatever the level, each diagram will contain from three to six boxes: this also has the effect of allowing the use of documents with a small format, which can be circulated within a team in order to gather comments according to a formalized procedure. The diagrams are then corrected on the basis of these comments and by cross-referencing between data modules and activity modules.

After approval by the decision-taking body, the mechanisms (machines or people) are put together by decomposing them down to the elementary level, the programs are written and SADT models are then used to produce the test package and the documentation.

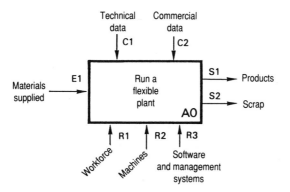

Fig. 6.15.
Simple statement of a typical SADT problem.

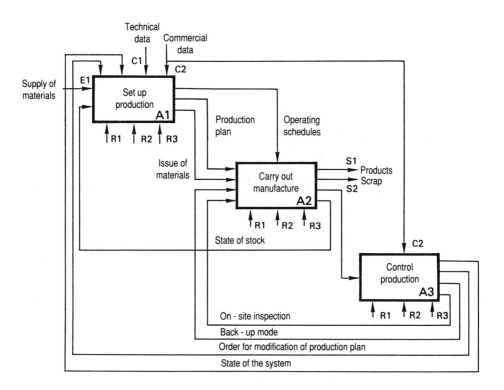

Fig. 6.16.
First-level decomposition of the A0 box of Fig. 6.15.

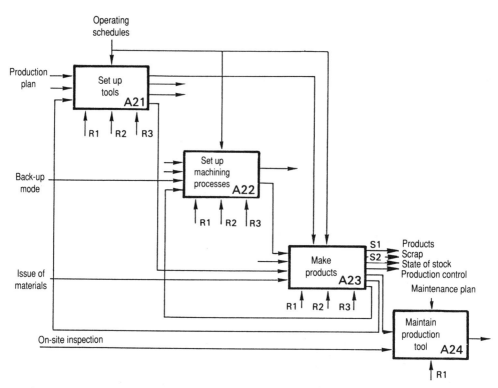

Fig. 6.17.
Second-level decomposition of the A2 box of Fig. 6.16.

6.4 TOWARDS SECOND-GENERATION INFORMATION TECHNOLOGY—THE KADS METHOD AND ARTIFICIAL INTELLIGENCE

6.4.1 Artificial intelligence and knowledge-based systems (KBSs)

The dream of making computers intelligent is one that has obsessed scientists and engineers since the very beginning of information technology. The long road to artificial intelligence, which (apart from research laboratories) began in the early 1980s, is now leading to increasing opportunities for the use of *knowledge-based information technology* in an industrial environment.

This is a promising area which embraces four main types of application:

(1) expert systems;

(2) pattern recognition (voice recognition, artificial vision);

(3) the understanding and processing of language;

(4) software engineering (putting the production and maintenance of software on an industrial footing).

These have the common feature that they model human reasoning and behaviour from a knowledge base containing the expertise of specialists or implicit knowledge that we all use (heuristic reasoning).

6.4.2 Expert systems

CIM projects are now introducing an increasing number of modules using KBSs, sometimes called 'second-generation systems'. The attractive feature of these new methods is that they replace traditional information technology when the solution to a problem relies exclusively on know-how that replicates the behaviour of human experts. In running industrial processes, for example, most systems make no use of artificial intelligence, but knowledge-based applications are now on the increase. There are two types of system to be considered.

One includes those that can be characterized by an exhaustive mathematical model, i.e. a set of transfer functions relating inputs to outputs. Running such processes then involves computer methods and depends on standard numerical algorithms. This is so, for example, in the case of nuclear reactors, where the very complex set of radioactive growths and decays forming the process concerned can be formally described by a set of mathematical laws governing the physical behaviour.

The other category includes the many systems whose mathematical formulation is incomplete, yet for which manual operation is often remarkably successful. Common-sense reasoning replaces the formal mathematical logic when the latter can no longer call on hypotheses and a total knowledge of what is involved. In this type of process, as in normal life, we have to face the problem of the limitations to our knowledge. Conclusions are continually being drawn without rigorous proofs as long as they appear plausible or 'reasonable'. Technology based on artificial intelligence is then a convenient means of simulating such behaviour. For example, our knowledge of the chemical and thermodynamic laws governing blast-furnace processes is still very incomplete, so that running such processes involves the second category of systems.

Running industrial processes using expert systems has only made its appearance recently because of its special features and its restriction to reasoning carried out in real time. Most expert systems now have the freedom to reason off-line (e.g. systems for diagnosis of breakdowns, simulation of scheduling, etc.).

Continuous reasoning on a dynamic system which is evolving with time puts restrictions on the performance which, although readily compatible with classical systems for running the process, come into conflict with the design requirements of an expert system. One precaution is then to divide the system into subsets, some of which can be dealt with by an efficient standard algorithm to respond to demands for rapidity of perception. The more conceptual levels of reasoning are then dealt with by 'expert' tasks whose time constraints become acceptable. However, there is still the need to ensure that the different parts are coordinated.

The concept of 'knowledge-based CIM' relies on a modular logical architecture which is a mixture of classical transactional algorithms with data-processing and KBSs. This allows a decentralized and cooperative approach to be adopted, which is advisable in view of the constraints of industrial responsiveness and operation in real time. This procedure also provides the possibility of implementing and testing the solution in stages.

Knowledge-based systems (KBSs) are no longer considered as ends in themselves, but rather as a method enabling particular problems to be solved and requiring the introduction of know-how or expertise into an information system.

Before describing the methods used to design this type of application, we first review some of the general ideas about the way in which expert systems operate.

An expert system consists of (1) a set of rules representing the area of expertise, forming what is called the *knowledge base*, and (2) an *inference engine*, governing the use of the rules. The inference engine (or interpreter of knowledge) is a program which draws its conclusions starting from data (taken as premises in the reasoning) and using the rules of the knowledge base. These conclusions are in their turn introduced into the knowledge base and can thus serve as the starting-point for new inferences (Fig. 6.18).

A rule is a situation–action pair, which means that every time a situation is recognized (left-hand part of the rule), the action is carried out (right-hand part of the rule). A rule-based system generally consists of three parts:

(1) the basic rules;

(2) the data structure or structures (basic facts) containing the known facts;

(3) the interpreter of the facts and rules, i.e. the mechanism which decides which rule is applicable and which triggers the corresponding action.

The facts and rules obey a syntax known to the interpreter or inference engine, which can then manipulate them logically, i.e. establish the truth or otherwise of certain assertions, establish new ones or eliminate them.

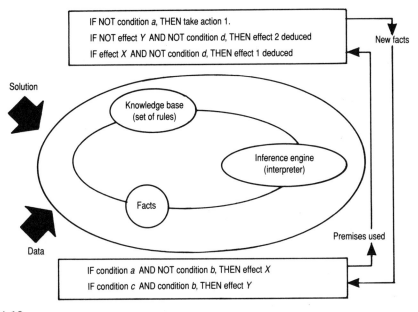

Fig. 6.18.
A knowledge-based system.

An expert system exploits data structures representing the knowledge acquired by human experts and simulates the function of these experts with a view to responding to the demand of a user. It is appropriate to separate the concerns of the expert system proper into two components: the solution of problems and the handling of dialogues with the user.

Problem-solving uses the expert knowledge to find the solution to a problem. The expert knowledge is represented as a set of collections of symbols in a knowledge base, manipulated by an inference engine that constructs the solutions to the problems.

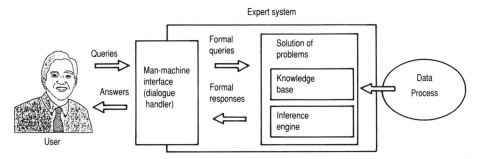

Fig. 6.19.
An expert system.

The problems are formulated as queries expressed in a formal language, and the solutions are reconstituted in the same language. To avoid the user having to conduct the dialogue in this formal language, a man–machine interface layer (the dialogue handler) acts as a mediator, translating the users' questions into formal queries and the formal responses into answers comprehensible to the users (Fig. 6.19).

6.4.3   The KADS methodology and the industrial development of expert systems

A study carried out in 1989 showed that the main reason why expert systems were not being used was an insufficiency of methods for development, especially in the construction of knowledge bases, i.e. the transfer of expertise.

Knowledge-based Systems Analysis and Design Support (KADS), originating in the European ESPRIT project P1098 and representing 75 man-years of work, is now one of the most highly developed KBSs. This pioneering method provides two types of support for the production of KBSs in an industrial approach: firstly, a life cycle enabling a response to be made to technical and economic constraints (control of the production process, quality assurance of the system, etc.), and secondly a set of models which structure the production of the system, especially the tasks of analysis and the transformation of expert knowledge into a form exploitable by the machine.

The KADS models

As in standard design methods, the KADS representation relies on a hierarchy of models (Fig. 6.20). The analysis phase is split into three main streams as follows:

(1) An external stream which identifies the constraints affecting the design and production of the system. This takes into account the effect of external specifications as in conventional systems.

(2) An internal stream which is concerned with the construction of the model representing the expertise proper.

(3) A modality stream involving the construction of a model of cooperation. This is the novel feature of the analysis phase in KADS: it involves formally taking user requirements into account by including factors such as the reaction to information technology, the context in which it

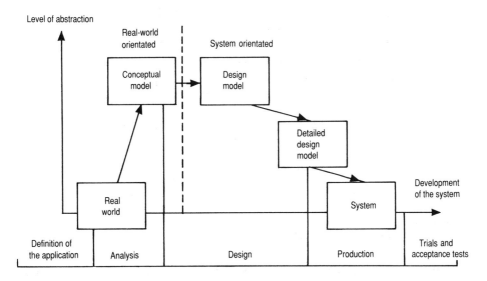

Level of abstraction

Fig. 6.20.
The hierarchy of models in KADS.

is used, any fears that are felt and by modelling scenarios for the use of the system-to-be.

The design phase of the system involves transforming the analysis model obtained as above into a global design model, the first stage in the construction of the operational system. This transformation process is very similar to that for a file of external specifications in the physical architecture used in traditional systems.

The global design model (Fig. 6.21) has three components which are produced in turn:

(1) *The functional model* specifies all the functions which the final system must contain. It thus includes a functional decomposition which specifies the interdependence of blocks such as 'is composed of', 'data flow', 'controls' and so on. The functional model reflects the external view seen by users of the system.

(2) *The behavioural model* explains how the functional blocks will be produced and is the starting-point for technical design. Each block is associated with a method of production. A method is defined through the components and the mechanisms it uses. For example, a method which uses an 'IF cause THEN effect' system of rules (classified under the term 'production system') distinguishes two main components: a

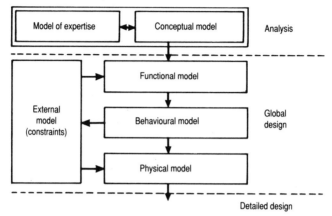

Fig. 6.21.
The global design model in KADS.

basic set of rules for production and an interpreter of the rules. This stage corresponds to logical design of data structures, of knowledge and of associated processes. The methods adopted characterize the behaviour of the system. In order to help the designer in this task, KADS provides a library of artificial intelligence techniques described in a uniform format.

(3) *The physical model* describes the architecture of the system-to-be in terms of the components required by the implementation of the methods described in the behavioural model.

The KADS four-layer model of expertise

The construction of the model of expertise is an essential task in the analysis stage. The aim is to provide a structure enabling the expertise to be represented. To achieve that:

(1) the modelling language must allow the semantics of the knowledge to be expressed (an unambiguous physical meaning for the knowledge as expressed by an expert);

(2) the proposed structure must be easily accessible to experts, particularly so that it can be validated;

(3) the results obtained must serve as a basis for the computerized design and production.

While problems are being solved, the experts are handling a highly diverse collection of knowledge. Expertise can be regarded as a hetero-

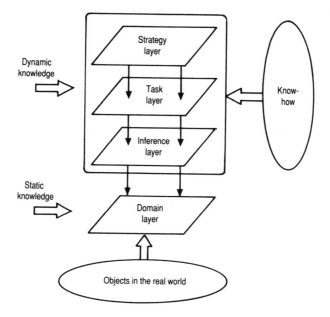

Fig. 6.22.
The KADS four-layer model of expertise.

geneous collection of interacting items of knowledge. The lack of a review stage very often observed in the analysis of KBSs is the source of many weaknesses: the analysis stage is not easy to control, the maintenance of knowledge bases is difficult, inconsistencies appear during the enrichment of the base and the performance deteriorates.

KADS proposes to structure the knowledge appropriately for any area of expertise using four layers of increasing abstraction (Fig. 6.22):

(1) *The domain layer*, i.e. a description of the world in terms of concepts (e.g. loss of charge in a blast furnace), relations between concepts (e.g. slipping is a cause of the loss of charge) and structures (e.g. cause and effect graph between primary causes and anomalies). This is expert knowledge. Separating static knowledge describing the semantics of the domain from its use is a necessary condition for flexibility in the use of the system and for the reuse of this knowledge.

(2) *The inference layer*, which describes the representation of the reasoning and the manipulation of the knowledge in the domain, such as the rules (e.g. hypothesis, conclusion), the sources of knowledge (e.g. selection) and the inference structures (e.g. diagnostics). These are the primitive elements of reasoning, i.e. the elementary processes trans-

forming existing information into new information. These various primitive elements are grouped together through inference structures which formalize a set of transformations in a given context for a precise objective.

(3) *The task layer*, which concerns the stages in the reasoning, the goals and the way of achieving them: a task structure (e.g. setting up). A task structure specifies how the inference structures are used to achieve a goal. Using an inference structure means specifying what path will be taken through it and what control elements are to be included. Several task structures may be combined in the same goal.

(4) *The strategy layer* describes the plan for solving the problem that is set and the knowledge required for its implementation (e.g. make an adjustment in the absence of an anomaly). This layer specifies the knowledge characterizing the behaviour of experts and its adaptation to the context of the problem. A plan for the solution schedules the goals to be achieved in order to solve the problem.

We mention once again the basic contribution of KADS in giving prominence to reasoning based on generic associations, i.e. models independent of a precise domain (e.g. a diagnostic model).

The SHELLEY cognitive engineering workbench

Associated with the KADS method is a software package known as SHELLEY, which provides an integrated set of software tools facilitating the development of KBSs in the analysis and design stages and in the running and monitoring of projects. The computer environment is properly integrated since the various facilities use the same object-oriented basis and each facility can call on the relevant tools according to the context.

Being similar in philosophy to CASE, the SHELLEY workbench is at the same time a procedural editor enabling interviews to be analysed, a design editor, a facility for modelling relationships, a library of models of certain reasoning strategies (generic models) and a library of methods derived from artificial intelligence.

7 The Financial Return from a CIM Project

7.1 ARE COMPUTER-AIDED SYSTEMS WORTHWHILE?

The question might well be raised as to whether it is always advisable to resort to computer-aided techniques like CAD, CAM and all the other systems that are usually shortened to the CA-X form. Is it not simply that we find it intellectually satisfying to imagine that there is a wealth of new applications replacing humans in their work, or are there commercial reasons? Is the financial return from investment in such systems always certain to be a positive one? Does not the intellectual pleasure gained from an escape into dreams of futuristic projects that are closer to science fiction than to economic reality often push the theoretically minded to extremes?

The classic rules of a market economy enable manufacturers of computers and peripheral equipment to profit from this enthusiasm by offering techniques with an ever-growing thirst for processing power and memory capacity, and this in turn leads to a continual increase in users' needs. Nevertheless, there is an economic basis for such an inflation in automated processes, even if it is not clearly evident from the viewpoint of the financier.

An example will illustrate this. If manual operation of telephone communication were still being used, we should need to employ half the population of the planet to handle all the calls currently being made. Now apply this argument to the production of software. Extrapolation of our present requirements in the processing of information to the end of the century (communications, banks, media, industry, administration, etc.) means that the whole world population ought by then to be engaged in the tasks of analysis and programming. Since this is an unlikely outcome, and since the growth in our requirements is inescapable, automation of program generation becomes the only practical way out. Of all the computer-aided systems, however, software engineering and now cognitive engineering (i.e. 'intelligent' systems for creating data-processing applications) are undoubtedly the sectors of present-day technology which are least widely used yet have the greatest thirst for processing power. This leads us to pose the question, 'What efforts should we agree to make today to ensure that we are competitive tomorrow?'

The answer may well lie in our thinking of CIM, like biotechnology and the new generation of materials, as a 'seed-corn technology' contributing to a transformation and development of the 'harvest technology' that forms the very basis of the main products in our economy (cars, aircraft, electronic equipment, chemicals).

There was a 'laboratory' period when companies investing in computer-aided production were heavily subsidized by governments. However, although this technology, hitherto the prerogative of very large companies, can in future be used by the majority of industries, they now have to provide the funds themselves.

7.2 INVESTMENT DECISIONS

Business managers are faced with investment decisions whenever the capacity and structure of the equipment or organization no longer match the realities of production and the current economic landscape.

Like all investment, committing capital to a project involving computer-based production is a risky operation, a bet on the future. Managers must have reliable criteria available to them on which they can base a decision. Wise investment will guarantee tomorrow's competitivity: a poor choice will put the future of the company in jeopardy.

Should investment be in proven technology or in new techniques? Is it not, even today, more profitable to invest in areas other than technological ones? Must we seek a rapid return (payback time less than two or three years) or would it, on the contrary, be worth sticking to a long-term industrial strategy?

It is rare for CIM to be implemented *en bloc* unless it is involved in the construction of a new production unit. In most cases a master plan will be drawn up so as to include a scenario for the overall restructuring of the organization of every unit in the company, and the development of the information systems belonging to the unit. This will enable the modular, yet general, approach of CIM to be adopted.

A certain number of projects will be integrated in this overall strategy: these are identified and each of them subjected to a feasibility study. However, isolated analysis of every project will lead to an underestimate of the overall profitability, since no account is then taken of the synergy brought about by project integration. A special feature of investment in computer-based production is its connection with the working environment (e.g. the integration of CAD and CAM quoted in Chapter 2).

One of the main difficulties in carrying out an *a priori* analysis of the return from an investment in CIM lies in this synergic effect. However, if the cost–benefit analyses of all the projects *assessed in isolation* are combined and found to lead to the conclusion that they are profitable, it is clear that the overall profitability of the integrated projects will have been broadly established.

Another major difficulty arises from the *a posteriori* measurement of benefits in an environment perpetually disturbed by external factors (markets, mobility of the workforce, replacement of production units). When a variation in productivity or in profits occurs, it is extremely difficult to discover how much of the change is due to the project itself and how much to external factors.

7.3 EVALUATION OF INVESTMENT PLANS

The first step in making an investment decision is knowing how to evaluate a project, i.e. how to describe its characteristics from technical and economic viewpoints. Implementing a new system will change the quantities both of the materials and resources used in production and of the products manufactured.

These changes will be experienced while the system is running, i.e. over several years. The outgoings that the company must face and the receipts it might hope to achieve will therefore be affected, and it is this variation in cash flow which enables an investment plan to be evaluated.

Suppose that a new system is put into service in the year 0. Its use during a later year t brings additional receipts r_t *and causes additional costs* c_t. This results in a change in gross profit of

$$p_t = r_t - c_t.$$

The terms r_t and c_t are positive (receipts and costs), but may be negative (loss of profit, or savings on another production factor).

Suppose we draw up a 'billbook' of receipts and costs. The series of gross profits $p_t = r_t - c_t$ will have the general shape shown in Fig. 7.1 for a start-up date at year 0 (the time-scale is not meant to be generally applicable but is merely an illustration).

Phase 1 corresponds to the setting up of the system. Its duration depends on the type of investment. The installation of a CAD system can be achieved in a few weeks, including user training, whereas a computer-

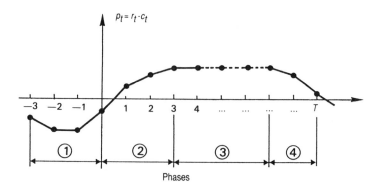

Fig. 7.1.
A sequence of gross profits year by year.

based PIC project might need several years. This stage comprises outgoings c_t only, and no receipts. For some systems these outgoings will be limited to c_0, the cost of equipment. In other cases, we shall proceed as if the costs were concentrated in a single value at the start-up date, with a modification which depends precisely on the criterion adopted for the choice of investment. This will then be called the investment cost I.

Phase 2 represents the rise when the system is running (becoming acclimatized to a CAD/CAM system, and capitalizing on the increasing experience with the system, progressive implementation of the various functions in a computer-based PIC system, etc.). The operation of the system under nominal conditions (phase 3) is generally characterized by regular gross profits, perturbed by various external factors such as changes in the market. With computer-based production equipment being introduced at the lower levels (machines), the perturbation could arise from internal factors (e.g. decennial revision, preventive maintenance, breakdowns).

The last phase (4) illustrates the end of the system's life. In CIM, an application will be abandoned due to obsolescence (new and much more efficient and competitive technology) and to equipment wearing out (more frequent breakdowns or more expensive upkeep). At date T, any possible decommissioning costs (e.g. dismantling of physical equipment, retraining of staff) and recovery values (e.g. sale of second-hand machines) are taken into account. The fact that projects leading to CIM are often still experimental in character makes it particularly difficult to estimate the date T and even more to estimate the costs and residual profits. Nevertheless, an objective study of the return on such a project must take into account the eventual abandonment of the system, however artificial this may seem.

The decision-maker is then faced with several problems:

(1) What is the optimum start-up date for the application?
(2) How can a system which proves to be timely be 'dimensioned' (what performance can be expected, what quantitative characteristics are required)?
(3) How can a choice be made between two projects using different methods to attain the same objective?
(4) More generally, how can a choice be made between different projects which do not exactly fulfil the same needs? In particular, since doing nothing is a sort of project, is it necessary to invest in a new system or would it be better to rely on the *status quo*?

For each of these questions, we have to compare the billbooks of the competing investments. This will involve comparing the series of flows relating to each project (collecting together the expenses prior to the date 0 in the investment cost I). How, for example, can we compare the following series for two projects A and B:

$$(-I_A, p_{A1}, p_{A2}, \ldots, p_{AT_A}) \quad \text{and} \quad (-I_B, p_{B1}, p_{B2}, \ldots, p_{BT_B})?$$

In the ideal case in which the investment cost of A is lower than that of B, in which A's gross profits always exceed those of B and in which its useful life is longer, it is obvious that project A will be the more profitable (see Fig. 7.2: cheaper, greater yield and longer lasting).

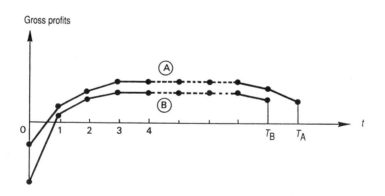

Fig. 7.2.
The gross profits for project A are always higher than those for B and it has a longer useful life: the choice is easy.

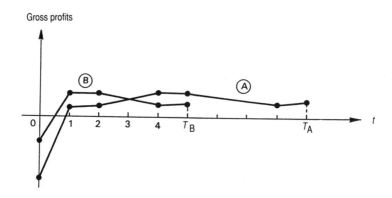

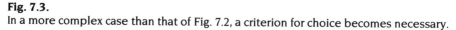

Fig. 7.3.
In a more complex case than that of Fig. 7.2, a criterion for choice becomes necessary.

In general, however, the choice is not as easy as that. In computer-based production, it is often a greater initial effort which is the source of higher and longer-lasting profit margins at a later date (Fig. 7.3). It is then no longer possible to settle the matter absolutely and a criterion for the choice becomes necessary. Establishing such a criterion amounts to comparing the sequences of outgoings and receipts by expressing them in a consistent form.

Before continuing with our study of the criteria most commonly used in taking decisions about investment in CIM technology, we must pin down the subject of our discussion more precisely. This does not mean that we need to review the general principles of a course in business economics, but rather that we must adapt and apply these principles to the special case of computer-integrated production. The following points are made with this in mind:

(1) We shall not be dealing with the responsibility connected with investment decisions or funding, i.e. with the question of how the capital required for achieving the anticipated investment can be obtained without compromising profitability, without the risk of seeing the company no longer able to face its financial obligations and without seeing the creditors interfering too much in internal management. This is a managerial matter which lies too far outside the specific area of CIM to be dealt with here.

(2) The fact that the information technology universally present in CIM applications becomes very quickly out of date, and that there is a

resultant increase in maintenance costs, leads us to take as a unit of measurement common to all cash flows that of the constant pound sterling at year 0.

The billbooks showing the variation in receipts and payments established on such a basis removes the effect of inflation by taking into account the relative changes (or drifts) in prices (running costs and receipts).

We recall that, if b is the general rate of increase or rate of inflation, h is the nominal rise in prices of an article and d is the rate of relative drift in the price of this article, we can write

$$1 + d = (1 + h)/(1 + b).$$

In order to have billbooks in constant pounds sterling, it is therefore sufficient to predict relative drifts d without the need to provide a forecast for the rates b or h. Estimates of the relative drift rates, which are quite closely linked to variations in the scarcity of goods and to the relative strengths of economic factors, are more accessible than estimates of the inflation rate (fall in the purchasing power of money) and the rates of nominal rises in the price of goods. Note also that the technological development of data-processing tools frequently leads to negative rates of drift in the calculation of CIM investments.

(3) The investor more particularly concerned with assessing productivity might sometimes find it an advantage to use constant prices, i.e. taking into account only a general rise in prices without being concerned with relative drifts between goods.

It is thus easier, in considering the variation in company receipts and expenditure, to take account of what can be attributed to the variation in prices (and hence the result of market forces) and what to the variation in quantities or volumes manufactured (due to improvements in production efficiency).

(4) Some opinions and theories put forward in the 1980s (e.g. those of Kaplan, Riggs, etc.) judge the traditional criteria of profitability as totally unsuitable for the evaluation of modern production systems since they do not take sufficient account of the effects of the synergy due to integration. These purely theoretical truths, which are often very difficult to apply in practice, do not invalidate the traditional methods of assessment recommended here: the latter are, after all, very well understood by industrialists and enable comparisons to be made with traditional investment.

Payback time

This is very simply the time required to pay back the initial investment *I* given by the sum of the agreed costs during the setting-up period. This time T_p is given by

$$\sum_{t=1}^{T_p} (r_t - c_t) = I.$$

The criterion associated with this value involves choosing the investment with the shortest pay-back time. If the following expression:

$$\sum_{t=1}^{t=n} ((r_t - c_t) - I) = P(n)$$

for two competing projects A and B is plotted graphically, curves with the general shape shown in Fig. 7.4 are obtained. Project A appears preferable to project B ($T_{pA} < T_{pB}$), whereas it is quite clear that the latter promises large profits in the long term. This criterion takes no account of differences in the useful life, nor of profits after the pay-back time has elapsed. It favours the short-term somewhat to the detriment of long-term investment.

Recovery of capital is a concept quite dear to decision-makers since it allows a simple evaluation of the future prospects of an investment and

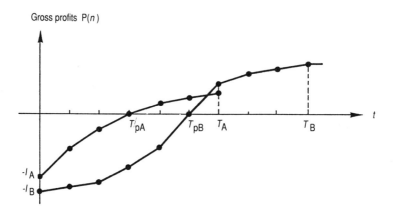

Fig. 7.4.
The gross profits for two projects A and B (see text).

Table 7.1
Typical times for recovery of capital

Technology	Pay-back time
Computer-based production and inventory control (essential functions, medium-sized firms)	1–2 years
Computer-based production and inventory control (extended functions, large firms)	2–4 years
Computer-aided design (CAD)	1–4 years
Computer-aided manufacturing (CAM)	1–3 years
Automated warehouse	1–3 years
Computer numerically-controlled machine tools (CNC machine tools)	2–3 years
Flexible workshop	3–7 years

thus of the risk in committing capital to a project. Some typical pay-back times are listed in Table 7.1.

Internal rate of return (discounted cash flow rate)

In spite of appearances, the above criterion is not only of concern for the simple recovery of an investment. At the very outset, it is clearly understood that an investor will wait for a short time after this pay-back period to gain additional profits. It is in the light of that, and of the probable useful life of the system, that the pay-back time will be judged to be acceptable or not.

We can therefore consider the inclusion of the whole period during which the system is running in looking for a greater profitability than the simple recovery of capital. This criterion is expressed in the form of a ratio between the mean gross profit and the level of investment:

$$\sum_{t=1}^{t=T} \frac{p_t}{TI} \, .$$

This procedure takes no account of the way in which the profits are spread out over time. The result would be unchanged if they were received in a different order, unlike the situation with the previous criterion.

An additional return will then be demanded in comparison with simple recovery. If this additional rate is r and if I is the initial funding, it would be necessary to recover profits p_t such that

$$\sum_{t=1}^{t=T} \frac{p_t}{(1+r)^t} + \frac{V_T}{(1+r)^T} = I,$$

where V_T is the balance of the pay-back values and the decommissioning costs. The internal rate of return r is the highest rate of profit that can be obtained from the operation. We might require of an investment project that its rate is above a minimum threshold profitability.

Discounted cash flow

Since the calculated value must be above a fixed value, why not use this directly (the previous calculation of an internal rate of return requires the solution of an equation of the Tth degree)?

If a is the given minimum threshold profitability, the discounted cash flow at rate a is defined by

$$\sum_{t=1}^{t=T} \frac{p_t}{(1+r)^t} + \frac{V_T}{(1+r)^T} - I = P(a),$$

where p_t is positive in general and $P(a)$ is a decreasing function of a, so that

If $a < r$, then $P(a) > P(r) = 0$.

Validating a project when the discounted cash flow at a rate a is positive is equivalent to seeking a rate of return r greater than a. The discounted cash flow $P(a)$ at rate a is determined in this way, a being the discount rate. The rate $a\%$ corresponds to the interest it is necessary to pay to the lender, to the dividend to be paid to the shareholders, to the minimum rate of return which can be guaranteed to investors if they possess the capital.

The notion of discount rate defined here (rate a comparable to a rate of return in constant pounds sterling) should not be confused with the term *capitalization* or *updating* sometimes used in the revision of contracts (the nominal rate of price rise h of an article), which should also be called *indexation*.

Application to the case of investment in CAD

Imagine a CAD project with investment costs of £0.1 million (hardware, software and user training). The typical useful life of such a system can be estimated at between five and seven years. Consider the most restrictive case, i.e. $T = 5$ years and a residual value of zero at the end of its life $(V_T = 0)$.

If the running costs of the system (excluding wages) amount to £42 000 for the production of 2000 drawings, the *pro rata* cost will be £42 000/2000 drawings, i.e. £21/drawing.

Table 7.2
Comparison of costs in drawing plans (a) manually, (b) using CAD

	Manual	**CAD**
Labour	4 hours × £18/hour = £72	2 hours × £18/hour = £36
Cost of CAD system	£0	£21
Total cost	£72	£57

Let us draw up the balance sheet between a manual setting up of the documents and automation by CAD as in Table 7.2. With the computer-aided method, the return achieved is £15/drawing, or £15 × 2000 drawings = £30 000/year. Fixing a minimum threshold rate of return of 8.5%, the discounted cash flow P $(a = 8.5\%)$ is given by

$$\sum_{t=1}^{t=5} \frac{30}{1.085^t} - 100 + £18\,200.$$

We can thus anticipate a return on the capital of

$$£18\,200/£1 \text{ million} = 18.2\%.$$

7.4   COSTS AND BENEFITS OF AN MRP2 SYSTEM

To make an estimate of the costs of an MRP2 type of integrated production system can require extremely detailed work. Nevertheless, the task is still easily carried out. The main items to be evaluated are as follows:

(1) the hardware (initial set-up and development);
(2) the software (or the cost of analysis and development of a possible specific application—estimate not so easy);
(3) the adaptation or additional development;
(4) training or advisory assistance (external);
(5) internal tasks (data-processing and user services).

On the other hand, it is rather more difficult to estimate the benefits. These are generally expected to be accounted for by the following:

(1) a reduction in stocks or articles in process of manufacture;
(2) an increase in productivity (mainly of indirect personnel);
(3) an improvement in customer service (reduction of lead times);
(4) better general management.

It is by no means rare to find that the benefits and improvements are very often created at points where they were not anticipated in the initial stages (see Sec. 3.1). Many companies have achieved the expected high performance as regards stock management, but have also improved the quality of customer service (which is difficult to predict in advance).

The implementation of a computer-integrated PIC system can always be justified financially. The benefits are created by the simplification of administrative procedures introduced in order to ensure a high degree of responsiveness, by the 'quality' aspect which it becomes possible to monitor throughout the manufacturing process, and by the possibility of an overall check on the company which hitherto had been impossible because of the cumbersome nature of the procedures.

An analysis of the return from CIM could take on the following basic structure:

(1) collect data typical of the present situation;
(2) identify the sectors to be improved;
(3) describe the improvements to the system in the sectors in question;
(4) estimate the annual profits;
(5) evaluate the costs (initial and annual);
(6) determine the payback time.

Such assessments require a knowledge of certain key figures, among which are the following:

(1) The annual sales (turnover, cost of sales, gross margins).

(2) The inventories (finished and semi-finished products, raw materials, products in process of manufacture).

(3) The holding cost rate.

(4) Annual labour costs (direct workforce, managerial staff, supervisory staff, warehouse staff, research and development, methods office, finance and accounts, marketing, sales).

(5) The annual cost (annual purchases).

(6) The materials/workforce ratio.

Note on the calculation of the holding cost rate

In general (see Sec. 3.3), stocks and products in process of manufacture are there to supply line or batch production. Keeping items in stock is therefore a costly necessity for the company and should not be considered as a misfortune.

In 1986, the rate of financing of a stock, i.e the sum of the storage costs and the interest rate, represented 15–25% of its value, e.g. at 25%, £0.1 million of stock costs £1000 per day.

Consider stock of value V (£ million) and annual related costs of C_1 for storage, C_2 for warehouse maintenance, C_3 for energy, and C_4 for losses and so on, all in £m. Denote the total annual cost of storage $C_1 + C_2 + C_3 + \ldots + C_n$ by C. Referred to the initial value of the stock, C is $100C/V = x\%$.

In addition, because of its immobilization, the capital V is subject to an interest rate of $y\%$, so that the total cost of possession is

$$V(1 + x/100)(1 + y/100) = V(1 + (x + y + xy)/100)$$

or, to the second order, $V(1 + (x + y)/100)$. We call $x + y = t\%$, the holding cost rate and the total amount is the holding cost.

Suppose that there is at present a stock worth £3 million and a holding cost rate of 25%. If it is possible to achieve a stock reduction of the order of 20%, there is a direct profit of 0.25×30 or £0.15 million. On the other hand, however, although it transparent to the financier (so that he is unaware of it), £0.6 million is released from the funds and could be invested in another project!

Appendix 1
CIM and Standardization

Modern production units are characterized by a proliferation of data-processing systems which have frequently been developed in an anarchic way, neglecting problems of communication between applications and of consistency of data.

A fundamental objective of CIM is to propose a standard model for integration of generic applications which are features of manufacturing companies. Such a unifying process must clearly be achieved through the establishment of a certain number of standards and norms which are the responsibility of different international organizations.

Without attempting to make an exhaustive list of all the work now in progress, it seems worthwhile giving a brief introduction to several organizations which are collaborating in working out standards in this field, together with an indication of the most representative elements of standardization which should one day converge towards an ideal model. We describe in turn:

(1) The European ESPRIT program, especially the projects involving CIM (the CIM–OSA model, the CNMA project and the MAP 3.0 standard).
(2) International's CAM-I.
(3) Data transfer standards in CAD graphics (IGES, VDA, SET, STEP).
(4) The EDI data interchange standard (EDIFACT).

The ESPRIT Project

The European Strategic Programme for Research and Development in Information Technology (ESPRIT), was set up in 1984 on the initiative of the European Commission. The project has three main objectives:

(1) Making available to European data-processing industries the basic technology for ensuring that they remain competitive in the 1990s.

(2) Promoting industrial cooperation in Europe in the field of information technology.

(3) Opening the way to setting up standards.

The agreed investment for the first tranche of the ESPRIT project amounted to 1500 Mecu (million ecus), half of which was provided by the EC with the other half being supplied by the industries participating in the programme. In order to complete the work undertaken in the programme, a follow-on project, ESPRIT II, was begun in 1988 with an allocated sum of 3200 Mecu and the same method of funding as before.

The world market for CIM-associated technology was 30 Gecu in 1986 and this should double by 1992: the European Community has 20% of the market at present. CIM is included in the four lines of research in the ESPRIT II programme, and 42 new projects with a CIM context have been undertaken.

CIM–OSA (Open Systems Architecture) (ESPRIT project 688)

The aim of the CIM–OSA project, known as AMICE (European CIM Architecture) in the ESPRIT programme, is to define a standard for the open architecture of CIM systems through a set of concepts and rules facilitating the setting up of a computer-integrated manufacturing environment.

CIM–OSA consists of a list of models with complementary references enabling the requirements of a company as regards organization, data processing and human and material resources to be synthesized. The design of the CIM system to be installed is deduced directly from the model formed in this way.

The infrastructure of the system will be based on ISO–OSI standards (International Standards Organization–Open Systems Interconnection), which define the standard for communication between information systems. As a result, CIM–OSA appears to be a perfect complement to the MAP standard (CNMA or Communications Network for Manufacturing Applications—ESPRIT project 955).

CIM–OSA will make fundamental contributions to the development of international standards in the CIM field. The ISO TC 184 standard already refers to the structure of the model advocated by CIM–OSA.

CNMA (ESPRIT project 955) and the MAP 3.0 standard

The inability of disparate equipment to communicate with each other in the 1980s led General Motors and Boeing to describe and develop the

Manufacturing Automation Protocol (MAP) and Technical and Office Protocol (TOP) programs respectively. These standards are based on the reference model for OSI (Open Systems Interconnection) defined by the International Standards Organization (ISO).

In 1985, on the initiative of the Commission of the EC and the European Map Users Group (EMUG), a European contribution to these standards was created, embodied in the CNMA project. CNMA is concerned both to be compatible with MAP and to complete it by integrating in it the specific features of industries that will make it into a standard in the wider sense. The project takes into account the recommendations of the ISO–OSI model, particularly the higher layers 6 (presentation layer) and 7 (application layer).

During the last few years, MAP has appeared in various international guises on the initiative both of the USA and Europe (NCC in 1984, AUTOFACT in 1985, CIMAP in 1986 for MAP 2.x, the Hanover trade fair in 1987 for MAP CNMA). The MAP 3.0 version was introduced during the Enterprise Networking Event (ENE '88) at Baltimore in 1988.

The CAM–I association

Computer-aided Manufacturing–International (CAM–I) is a non-profit-making international association funded by large industrial groups. The organization is involved in research and development of computer-integrated production methods. Like many similar organizations such as the Manufacturing Studies Board of the National Academy, the National Science Foundation and the ESPRIT programme, CAM–I is committed to the principle that only companies which use CIM effectively will survive international competition in manufacturing industry. The projects it has currently in progress involve:

(1) solid modelling in CAD;
(2) applications of artificial intelligence to manufacturing production (scheduling etc.);
(3) planning of production processes;
(4) quality;
(5) the architecture of CIM and CIE (Computer-integrated Enterprise) systems;

At present CAM–I is particularly concentrating its effort on this last aspect in an attempt to reply to the question 'What efforts in time, resources and means must a company agree to in order to set up a CIM system?' Simply using the technology to automate manufacturing does not on its own justify the need for it: it must be possible to show that it is profitable. CAM–I proposes to define the bases for the measurement of profitability through the CMS (Cost Management System) and CIE projects.

Data exchange standards in CAD graphics

In the absence of a universal format for CAD/CAM, industries have opted for many systems each with their advantages and deficiencies: some software is recognized for its modelling facilities, some for its functionality in CAM and so on. Peugeot, for example, has chosen CADDS 4X (Computervision) for its bodywork plant and Catia (Dassault System) for its mechanical plant, while Renault has adopted Euclid–IS software (Matra Datavision). The research departments of subcontractors, increasingly involved in the definition or mechanization of components, must be capable of using CAD or CAM data from, and sending it to, the customers to whom they supply orders.

Exchange standards in CAD satisfy a dual need: the exchange of data between differing CAD/CAM systems and the storage of information in a neutral form. If these standards are to be universally applicable, they have to be constantly evolving and enriched by new ideas, yet the resulting adaptations and changes which are a permanent feature of them must not obscure another basic requirement: their stability over long periods of time. As a standard evolves, it should remain compatible with itself.

This dilemma explains the disordered growth in the software enabling a dialogue to be established between two dissimilar systems. As new versions come along, they are given additional functions until the product becomes too cumbersome to use and is abandoned in favour of a new one built on a sounder basis. This is one of the rules that determines the life cycle of software in general.

The first generation of graphics data exchange programs incorporated channels enabling a dialogue to be established between CAD systems in pairs (Fig. A.1.1(a)), by transcription of one proprietary database in its native format into the other. Although this method of code transfer had undeniable advantages such as speed, reliability and no risk of misinterpretation, its weaknesses opened the way to the first standards advocating the use of a neutral format (Fig. A.1.1(b)).

The data exchange standards, IGES, SPAC, VDA and, very shortly, STEP, aim to facilitate the transfer of data between incompatible CAD/CAM systems while guaranteeing the durability of the corporate databank, which cannot be linked to the particular choice of applications software.

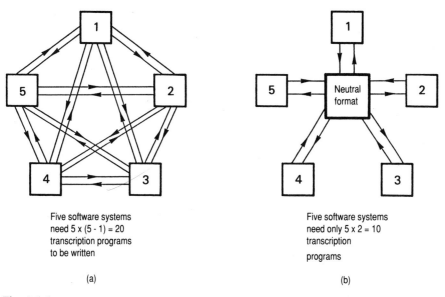

Five software systems
need 5 x (5 - 1) = 20
transcription programs
to be written

(a)

Five software systems
need only 5 x 2 = 10
transcription

programs

(b)

Fig. A.1.1.
(a) First-generation graphics data exchange programs established dialogues between CAD systems in pairs; (b) the neutral format enables the number of transcription programs to be reduced.

The life expectancy of the company's thesaurus is very much longer than that of the system that has been used to create it.

The data exchange standard (IGES)

Initial Graphics Exchange Specification (IGES) can be considered as the first standard for the exchange and storage of CAD data. It first appeared in the USA in 1979 and has been an ANSI standard since 1981.

It is based on a very simple principle, the concept of a neutral format. Each CAD application is provided with two translators each able to transcribe in both directions the contents of the internal database in a format that is completely specified and universally known. This neutral format is one that copes with descriptions of complex volumes and surfaces, assemblies, modes of projection and so on, and is very different in kind from that associated with standards for geometrical description such as GKS, CGM or HPGL: these are only able to handle elementary forms (e.g. text, points, segments, arcs).

IGES has been considerably enriched since the 1.0 version dating from 1980. From the simple geometrical description of elementary components, it has taken on board specifications of 3D forms of the CSG (constructive solid geometry) type. This has been achieved by incorporating, as it evolved, finite element mesh generation, specifications relating to AEC fields (architecture and engineering) and the concept of connectivity, which is fundamental to schematics.

The IGES 4.0 version handles non-geometrical entities such as annotating and dimensioning. The 5.0 version will support the B-Rep (boundary representation) type of description and scale information.

IGES is now included in almost all CAD packages, but it is beginning to suffer from old age. Its bases have become obsolete in spite of continuous updating, since they were fixed when it was first created. It has a fixed format in ASCII code in which unused spaces are filled with 'blanks', and it leads to an enormous wastage of space in memory and long transfer times. An IGES file is some 10 times larger than the original file, and a complicated index and poor optimization of data storage affects the read/write times. The complexity of IGES, which deals with more than 190 different entities, should also be mentioned and the fact that a given CAD system uses only a small proportion of them has led to the definition of subsets of the standard.

The German exchange format (VDA)

The VDA (Verband der Automobil) format was created by the German automobile industry. It is mainly concerned with the use of high-order polynomials to model complex curves and surfaces like those involved in the bodywork of cars. Its success (it is still used by German manufacturers) can be attributed to its very specialized nature. VDA, a DIN standard, is divided into two branches: the original standard, VDA-FS, and a more efficient product, VDA–IS, which has become a subset of IGES.

SPAC from Citroën and UNISURF from Renault are French versions of VDA that were used by the first CAD software packages for the car industry. They now have to replace this by the SET format.

The French exchange format (SET)

Standard d'Echange et de Transfert (SET) was developed on the initiative of the aerospace industry from 1983 onwards. The project was motivated by the weaknesses observed in the standards existing up till then. However, although inherently more efficient than its elders, SET has had little success outside France and is still almost unknown in US industry.

The year 1990 could be the decisive one for SET: it is used in the European Airbus and Hermes programmes and the French car industry has made it their spearhead. Partners in the national automobile world, forced to equip themselves with SET translators, could in their turn promote this standard.

SET is more precise and more homogeneous than IGES and has two main advantages: it covers all the functionalities of the CAD systems now on the market and it offers the capability of self-enrichment when any new idea comes along. These features rely on the use of dictionaries (sets of predefined parameters which can be assigned to a block of information) and of libraries (sets of external data to which SET can refer).

The international standard (STEP)

Standard for Exchange of Product Data (STEP) is an international initiative whose objective is the emergence of a universal standard governing the dialogue between different CAD systems. It is a project which combines the main standards at present in use. It was launched by the ISO in 1983 and is not expected to be finished before 1992, which explains why there is an intermediate generation of standards being used today as a substitute. Two of the main representatives of such preliminary efforts, which have no claim to be standards, are Product Data Exchange Standard (PDES), a US contribution which is an enriched recasting of IGES, and CAD–I, research into which has been carried out since 1984 as part of the European ESPRIT programme ending in 1990.

Two concepts emerging from this work are worth special attention: the intelligent translation of geometrical data which could not be transmitted from one system to another, and the handling of exceptions.

Intelligent translation of geometrical data gives an interpretation of data transmitted from a high-quality system to one of lower quality: such an interpretation is degraded at the level of a true mathematical representation, but is a sound one at the practical level. For example, a 20-degree Bézier surface will be previously split into small 3-degree surfaces to be capable of assimilation by less powerful software. The division will be finer as the tolerance threshold falls. These algorithms for the reduction of the degree will be integrated into each translator.

The handling of exceptions involves extracting the greatest possible amount of information from a neutral file, especially when the file contains anomalies or entities unknown to the receiving software. Current translators operate on an all-or-nothing basis, i.e. the neutral file is either completely rejected or completely translated.

The data exchange standard (EDI)

We hardly need to point out that paper documents inhibit production flow, often require redundant processing, are the source of numerous errors and have a profound effect on indirect costs. Handling such documents is no longer compatible with the demands of speed and efficiency imposed by present-day industry, distribution and transport.

Electronic Data Interface (EDI) is a method of exchanging documents in electronic form directly between a computer and one or more other computers. The exchanges can take place either within one establishment or between different ones. Exchanges of information between departments or firms use assorted information systems, so that EDI has to combine the functions of translation (encoding to and decoding from a neutral format), storage and transmission.

EDI can be considered as the development from the movement towards integration of information systems that began in the 1960s. Later, with the emergence of transaction-oriented applications, system integration became the keyword. An ever increasing wish to communicate led to the germination of concepts such as CIM, in which 'islands of information' generally based on different equipment are consolidated into the interior of a powerful information system. In situations where, traditionally, it was *de rigueur* to use the telephone or postal system, EDI had to be imposed in order to facilitate communications.

EDI originated in the distribution sector of the USA. After its successful use in the agro-food industry, it gradually spread to other sectors of industry until between 20 and 25 industrial areas are now involved in the use of the standard. It is estimated that the EDI market will be about $1.9 billion by 1992.

The public EDI standard was developed to facilitate data exchange independently of their organizations, and of the communication systems and data-processing equipment being used. The standard provides a common format, thus avoiding the use of multiple proprietary formats between trading partners.

EDI is the subject of an ANSI project, ANSI ASC X.12 (Accredited Standards Committee X.12) and of a TDCC project (Transportation Data Coordinating Committee). These standards have been approved by the ISO. They define the elements of the elaboration of commercial documents in force in international exchanges between producers, distributors, importers, exporters, transport companies, financial organizations, customs and excise and any other administrative body.

Electronic Data Interchange For Administration, Commerce and Transport (EDIFACT) is the international standard ISO 9735, based on the standard ISO 7372 of the *Trade Data Element Directory*. ASC X.12 of ANSI is responsible for the promotion and support of the EDIFACT standards in the USA and Canada.

Appendix 2
Glossary of Terms and Abbreviations

The technology associated with CIM embraces a wide variety of disciplines and a correspondingly large number of terms and abbreviations. A short description of some of those used in the present book, and in the field generally, is given below.

Computer-aided design (CAD)

A set of data-processing techniques used for the design and development of products. It includes but goes beyond CADD (see below) in that it uses simulation techniques to model the physical characteristics of an object, while the ideas of CAD are extended still further in computer-aided engineering.

Computer-aided drawing and drafting (CADD)

A system enabling very detailed graphical models to be produced in interactive form. Drawings, plans, blueprints, etc. can be retrieved, duplicated, modified by using varying parameters, and so on. Complex objects can be created by assembling them from a 'library' of elementary graphical units. Two-dimensional (2D) systems, only providing for plane representations, are distinct from 3D systems in which several representations of the same graphical model can be drawn, e.g. various perspective views, cross-sections in various planes, etc. CADD is a part of the more general field of CAD.

Computer-aided engineering (CAE)

This is often confused with CAD, but is in fact an extension of it. There are now three main areas in which CAE can be applied:

(1) The prediction or simulation of performance by calculating the theoretical responses of dynamic, electronic or logic systems.

(2) The calculation of structures and the prediction of reliability, which involves the application of the laws of physical behaviour to a geometrical model provided by CAD (finite element modelling).

(3) The simulation of operational processes, involving the study of how a manufacturing process behaves by modelling it using state variables (simulation of scheduling; operational research).

Computer-aided maintenance

Machines and equipment (NC machine tools, large motors, compressors, PLCs, etc.) are nowadays fitted with localized or centralized sensors and monitoring systems designed to make it easy to maintain them. In a computer-aided maintenance system, a central supervisor monitors the production lines and records all events, thus forming a historical record from which it is possible to calculate the breakdown rate for the various components, the MTBF, the MTTR (see below), etc. Counters add up the number of cycles during which particular components are used and trigger an alarm when a change of tool or component becomes necessary. This is the start of conditional maintenance. The information stored in the system is then transferred to the following:

(1) The computer-aided maintenance control system, which centralizes it and provides for the management of the maintenance processes.

(2) Expert systems for diagnostic and quality control programs.

(3) Possibly a multi-media server which will provide the specialist in maintenance with a file of technical data needed for trouble-shooting (work sheets, warehouse dockets, diagrams, plans, photographs, etc.). In a CIM context, the technical data about workstations and equipment will be shared with the computer-based PIC system.

Computer-aided maintenance control (sometimes CAMC)

A system which centralizes the information from remote monitoring of machines and equipment and provides for their maintenance (see previous entry).

Computer-aided manufacturing (CAM)

The use of a computer to generate the data required to configure a production process, for example the parameters needed to set up NC machine tools and robots. The technique makes it possible to work out production schedules, simulate processes such as the movements of a machine tool during a machining operation, and download manufacturing programs to CNC machine tools (remote job entry).

Computer-aided software engineering (CASE)

A set of integrated facilities in information technology, supplemented by one or more methods for the specification and analysis of the projects to be computerized. It designs, produces and maintains application programs with a high level of rigour and as automatically as possible, using data dictionaries, automatic program generators, etc. The very costly toing-and-froing between the specification and production stages are reduced to a minimum, even possibly eliminated, while the resultant application programs are very easily maintained. Such systems should be able to increase the productivity of analyst-programmers and systems engineers by a considerable factor in the years to come.

Computer-integrated manufacturing (CIM)

The concept of a completely automated factory in which all the functions of a company (design and methods, production, administration, accounting, marketing, etc.) are integrated and controlled by computerized systems. CIM enables all those involved in the company to use common data shared through the same database, thus improving responsiveness and efficiency when faced with fluctuating markets.

Computer numerically controlled (CNC) machine tools

See NC below.

Database management system (DBMS)

A database is a set of files which can be accessed through different application programs. Each application can be considered as a channel by which information in the database can be sought and retrieved or updated. Each item of data only exists once in a database, but is accessible to any application. This 'uniqueness' of the data enables their integrity to be guaranteed whatever use is made of them. The DBMS is a logical layer between the application programs and the physical files: it translates the instructions for handling the data in the programs into physical input–output (I–O) operations on the files. Two main DBMS systems are recognized today:

(1) Navigational systems (hierarchical, network and CODASYL databases) in which the data are linked by a pointer mechanism, which is very efficient and guarantees an excellent level of security.

(2) Relational systems, whose data are structured into tables and which provide a high degree of flexibility in use.

Directly numerically controlled (DNC) machine tools

See NC below.

Finite element method (FEM)

The origins of structure calculations in mechanics go back to the last century with the theory of beams (St Venant, Castigliano, Navier, etc.). When matrix methods came on the scene, these techniques gave rise to the finite element method. The matrix approach to structure calculations involves:

(1) constructing local stiffness matrices (i.e. the elementary matrices expressing the force–displacement relationships at the nodes) after establishing the relationships between stresses and strains;

(2) transforming the matrices to a common frame of reference;

(3) combining them into a global stiffness matrix;

(4) solving the linear system of equations (matrix inversion) and thus obtaining the displacements at the nodes;

(5) calculating the loads and stresses in each component.

The FEM involves the extension of this principle to calculations with continuous media by dividing up the domain into as large as possible a number of subdomains of simple shape (triangles, rectangles, etc.). The form of such a discretization is obvious for beams, but in FEM a fictitious network of boundaries, and therefore nodes, is created, most of them having no physical significance. Instead of integrating the local equations of continuity and elasticity directly, the FEM progresses from one cell to another, using a limited expansion. In addition, by making an assumption about the form of the displacement field, we end up with a particularly simple type of calculation: the polynomial form.

Flexible manufacturing system (FMS)

A system controlled by a host computer which organizes the supply of materials, the programs for the NC machine tools, the tooling of machines, etc. in a highly flexible manner so that changes in the manufacture of parts and assemblies can take place without costly delays in retooling, recon-figuration, etc.

Fourth-generation language (4GL)

First-generation computer languages were binary in form, appropriate to the logical structure of the basic solid-state processors. The second genera-tion replaced each binary code (standing for instructions, operands, addresses, etc.) by a more meaningful mnemonic symbol. The third gener-ation became more remote from machine language and was structured using operations at the highest possible level. An instruction then very frequently consisted of a set of elementary machine operations (printing of a set of characters, loop structure, complex conditional jumps, etc.). The writing of such programs was certainly simplified but, in order to reply to a given question, the method of accessing the information had to be indicated by an algorithm (response to WHAT? and HOW?). Fourth-generation languages are very close to natural forms of communication. To obtain the required information, it is enough to specify what is sought (question WHAT?) without indicating the explicit method of access. We then speak of *assertional* languages, as opposed to *algorithmic* languages. It goes without saying that the increased ergonomic efficiency as the language generations succeed each other will be paid for by increasing demands on the storage capacity and processing power of computers.

Group technology (GT)

Group technology is by no means new. It involves the coding and classifi-cation of parts and their grouping into families. The underlying idea of this is to avoid 're-creating' already existing components and thus to reduce the number of plans and to standardize them, so improving manufacturing efficiency. Methods engineers also find the idea useful in facilitating scheduling and optimizing the use of tools. Typical ranges of parts can be defined in each family and the operator setting up machine tools no longer has to waste time carrying out tasks already performed in the past. GT also offers the possibility of creating 'manufacturing cells' dedicated to a family of parts, with all the advantages that such a system brings: better routeing of the parts, increased batch sizes, and so on. Computer-aided GT uses the technical database forming part of the computer-based PIC system.

Industrial LAN (ILAN)

See LAN below

Just-in-time (JIT)

A system of production in which a workstation receives the exact quantity or supplies needed at the right moment from the preceding workstation. JIT methods apply equally well to production processes (in workshops) and to supplies, and rely on a set of techniques (continuous flow production, reduction in tool-changing time, Kanban system) aimed at making the flow of materials and information as fluid as possible throughout the company. 'Reconstitution of consumption' methods like the Kanban system are in fact merely management procedures adapted to a JIT environment. Such methods by themselves cannot claim the advantages of a JIT system in a non-JIT environment.

Knowledge-based systems (KBS)

See sec. 6.4.

Local area network (LAN)

A means of communication between data-processing systems through a physical link of limited size. A local network is involved when the communication is between machines separated by anything from 10 m to several kilometres (between 10 cm and a few metres, communication is generally via a computer bus, and above 10 km long-distance networks are involved). Company LANs generally provide communication between company management systems and office automation systems (transfer of files between departments, exchanges between large servers, etc.). In a CIM environment, company LANs only occur at the highest levels of the overall system (at the company and factory level). They generally have large throughputs, from several Mbit/s to several tens of Mbit/s).

An industrial LAN (ILAN) is a special type of LAN providing a high level of immunity to interference in disturbed environments like workshops (from electromechanical disturbance, mechanical impacts on cables and connectors). A particular feature of ILANs is the diverse nature of the equipment involved in communication: computers, PLCs, CNC machine tools, sensors, actuators, etc. They must be absolutely reliable since they are the means by which data are transformed into mechanical work: any malfunctioning could put the worker at risk. A frequent requirement for ILANs is that they be capable of on-line maintenance (dynamic reconfiguration, starting up, etc.). The constraints from having to handle physical processes and from safety requirements generally mean that strict conditions must be imposed as regards responses (the system must take into account and process an item of data in a very short time, as in the case of an emergency stoppage or an alarm) and real-time performance (speed of sampling, feedback controls, etc). Throughputs of ILANs generally lie between 50 kbit/s and several tens of Mbit/s.

Master (production) schedule (MPS)

A facility for simulating the long-term planning requirements. Based on the 'game plan' of the company, it provides help in the decisions to be made when validating an operational manufacturing programme or when assessing investment in or reorganization of the means of production. A manufacturing programme validated through a master schedule is a contract between management and the representatives of the various functions in the company. In order to achieve an effective strategic plan, the technical data dealt with by the MPS come from the database of the computer-based PIC system and are gathered into coded groups, according to the rules for handling families (see GT). The MPS in this case is generally integrated into the computer-based PIC system.

Material requirements planning (MRP)

This is one of the basic methods of stock control. It has two logical steps:

(1) Simulation of the future stock position, calculated from its present positions, the potential incoming stock and the anticipated or firm outgoings of stock.
(2) The decomposition of the requirements over the lower levels of the bills of materials.

These two steps are repeated at each level of assembly from the finished products. The manufacturing and purchase orders are determined in this way from forecasts and customers' orders. Unlike the classic 'order point' method, which is based on the past by using historical records of consumption, MRP makes more use of present and future predictions to determine the requirements.

Manufacturing resource planning (MRP2)

An extension of the MRP concept, first to the planning of other resources (machine loads, staff loads, etc.), and later to the integration of several planning horizons, in the long term with the master schedule, in the medium term with manufacturing and supply programmes and in the short term with workshop scheduling and monitoring.

Mean time before failure (MTBF)

The mean time between breakdowns, enabling preventive maintenance to be programmed into the computer-aided maintenance system.

Mean time to repair (MTTR)

The combination of MTTR with MTBF gives rise to the idea of the availability of a machine or piece of equipment. This is essential to a realistic planning of manufacturing tasks and maintenance work. The availability ratio D is defined as MTBF/(MTBF + MTTR).

Numerically controlled (NC) machine tools

Numerical control involves a set of techniques for controlling machines using data in digital form (alphanumeric codes and various symbols) and recorded using a suitable medium (floppy discs, magnetic tape, punched tape, etc.), usually nowadays known as computer numerical control (CNC). When it is by direct link with a computer, it is said to be directly numerically controlled or DNC.

Production and inventory control (PIC)

A computer-based PIC system is designed to optimize the resources of the company (i.e. the financial resources, the materials, the work loads) for a given required volume of production. It takes into account the planning of the resources required for the production process and the monitors the way it is carried out. It includes a vast range of functions, from the elaboration of manufacturing programmes to the monitoring of workshop operations and covers all the coordinating activities such as the definition of the product structures (technical database of the bills of materials and manufacturing schedules), stock control, MRP calculations, purchasing, workshop scheduling, etc.

Programmable logic controller (PLC)

A data-processing system dedicated to the monitoring or control of actuators and sensors of physical magnitudes in an industrial environment (jacks, motors, limit switches, thermometric probes, etc.). PLCs were initially designed merely to replace wired logic systems, which were difficult to reconfigure. The development of microprocessors and the resultant increase in computing power has gradually extended the functions of PLCs to the handling of analogue variables, so that they occur in automatic control systems as PID controllers or as processors of signals representing raw data such as the magnitudes of physical quantities. PLCs form the 'lowest' layers of the CIM model (control of actuators such as jacks and motors, acquisition of physical quantities, control of robots, etc.).

Single minute exchange die (SMED)

A method combining several simple techniques for achieving a considerable reduction in tool-changing times (from several hours to a few minutes). Four steps are involved:

(1) a distinction between tasks which bring the station to a standstill and those which are external and can be carried out in parallel;
(2) an attempt to make internal tasks 'external';
(3) a reduction in internal tasks by rationalizing the setting up;
(4) rationalization of the external tasks.

Total quality control (TQC)

The object of this is to avoid any form of waste. It involves a state of mind based on the 'five zeros' approach (zero stock, defects, paper, breakdowns and lead time). In the context of information systems, it is recommended that quality control is integrated into the production process, thus allowing continual feedback to the manufacturing and supply processes and guaranteeing maximum responsiveness to untoward events. That is why TQC is generally combined with JIT.

Appendix 3
Case Study of a CIM Unit

A3.1   INTRODUCTION

The Bull factory at Villeneuve d'Asq, which assembles the Questar terminals and Zenith microcomputers distributed in Europe, was established in the 1980s. There were no design constraints as a result of any pre-existing plant, and the project was therefore able to take the opportunity of integrating the JIT concept into an environment that fully merited the CIM label.

The plant employs 350 people and benefits from a young and well-qualified staff: their average age is 32 and the machine operators all have technical diplomas or have passed the *baccalaureat*.

A3.2   STRATEGIC AIMS AND MAIN OPERATIONAL GUIDELINES

Efficiency and adaptability were the main objectives guiding the Bull management in their Villeneuve project. Efficiency was to be achieved by reducing the products in process of manufacture, by flexibility in production and by high quality. Adaptability involved progressively incorporating automation in the workstations as the production volume increased, a procedure that closely followed the development of Bull itself.

The objectives were translated into five operational guidelines:

(1) The introduction of automation into the flow of materials and parts from the reception of components and sub-assemblies and their transfer to pallets and stock boxes, right through to the arrival of the palletized finished products ready for dispatch to customers.

(2) Incorporation of the concept of quality at all levels ('no departures from specifications').

(3) Automatic monitoring of production over the whole process.

(4) Progressive automation of selected workstations in accordance with the increase in work loads and the availability of robotic systems.

(5) Integration of the following operations into the process: assembly, burning, testing and packaging.

A3.3   A MANAGEMENT INFORMATION SYSTEM ORGANIZED IN FIVE HIERARCHICAL LEVELS (Fig. A.3.1)

The information system at the plant is based on a five-level structure:

(1) MRP-type production control at the first level;

(2) Plant management based on JIT and process supervision;

(3) local PLCs;

(4) machine PLCs;

(5) transported information.

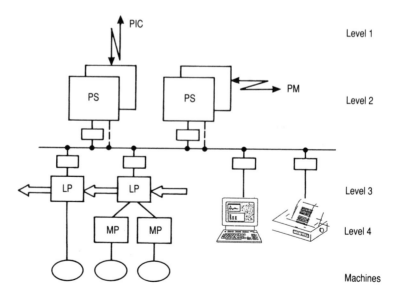

Fig. A.3.1.
The five-level structure of the information system: PIC = production control; PM = plant management; PS = process supervision; LP = local PLCs; MP = machine PLCs.

Level 1: Production control (PIC)

Production control at level 1 enables net requirements to be calculated according to MRP principles (see Chapter 4). Supplies are thus planned for the medium and long term, the forecasts being updated every week. The availability of components is monitored by daily checking.

Level 2: Plant management (PM) system

Following a JIT philosophy, PM works out the operational production programmes. Forecasts are updated daily. Monitoring of availability here is concerned with resources and equipment (workstations, machines, operators, etc.).

The level of detail in plant management and its area of application give this system control over the following activities: reception, manufacturing releases, production monitoring, movements of forklift trucks and dispatch.

Level 2: Process supervision (PS) system

It was also convenient to operate the PS system at level 2. This system controls and monitors the functioning of the automated equipment.

Level 3: Local PLCs (LP)

These control the operational equipment at the cell level and look after such large-scale functions as the choice of warehouse lane, the progress of conveyor trays, allocation of positions for palletizing.

Level 4: Machine PLCs (MP)

These control the elementary functions of machines and other equipment, and are coordinated with the local PLCs. For example, there will be one machine PLC per lane of the automatic warehouse, one machine PLC per wire-guided trolley, one machine PLC per transfer operation at workstations.

Level 5: Transported information

This includes the individual physical conveyors of information such as the labels on the pallets in reception, labels on the stock boxes of primary components, electronic badges under conveyor trays, labels on the boxes used for packaging, labels on the pallets in the dispatch section.

A3.4 THE OPERATIONAL SCENARIO

A3.4.1 Reception and initial inspection, transfer (Fig. A.3.2)

Reception

A check is made to see that the components received conform to those ordered. A bar-coded label is automatically issued by PM at level 2 for identification of pallets.

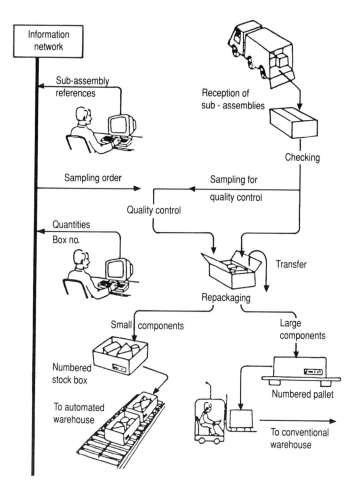

Fig. A.3.2.
Reception and inspection of incoming components and transfer to warehouses or stockboxes.

There are two possible destinations for pallets of components:

(1) 'Large' components are stored in a traditional warehouse controlled in real time by PM (PM terminal carried on forklift trucks).
(2) 'Small' components go to the transfer station to be stored there in standard stock boxes.

Transfer

The operator reads the bar codes on the pallets with an optical bar-code reader and then fills the stock boxes with the appropriate number of components (information specified on his PM terminal).

The operator reads the bar codes of each full stock box using an optical bar-code reader. The PM system identifies and memorizes the contents of each of these stock boxes.

A.3.4.2   **Storage and preparation** (Fig. A.3.3)

Conveyors are used to transport the boxes automatically from the transfer station to the automated warehouse (and to transport the empty boxes back to the transfer station). The automated warehouse stores the boxes and sends them back (first-in-first-out basis) as soon as the kitting stations ask for them.

Requests for large components are handled by PM, which then sends a message on the terminal carried on the forklift truck. The truck then looks for the pallet in question at the location indicated on its terminal and deposits it on a platform where it is automatically loaded on to a wire-guided trolley to be routed to its final destination.

The stock boxes emerging from the automated warehouse are carried by the same wire-guided trolleys to the kitting lines. The trolleys can carry four boxes or one pallet at a time.

A3.4.3   **'Kitting' and release** (Fig. A.3.4)

An operator now makes up a 'kit' by taking all the components required for the assembly of a product and putting them in a wooden box called a 'kitting box'.

As soon as an empty box of components is discharged from the previous stage, the kitting racks (incorporating all the references of the components used in the day's production) are automatically supplied by the automated

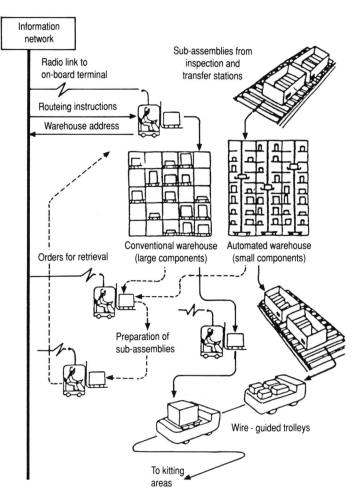

Fig. A.3.3.
Storage and preparation.

warehouse and wire-guided trolleys. The kitting box is positioned on a
conveyor tray carrying a magnetic memory.

Product release is created by the freeing of downstream workstations
(pulled flow) and in accordance with the production programme. It is
signalled by the arrival at the kitting station of a batch consisting of an
empty kitting box + conveyor tray, the memory on the tray having been
previously loaded with all the appropriate information (product reference,
series number, assembly schedule, etc.). Slips with the same information
are printed and fall automatically into the kitting boxes.

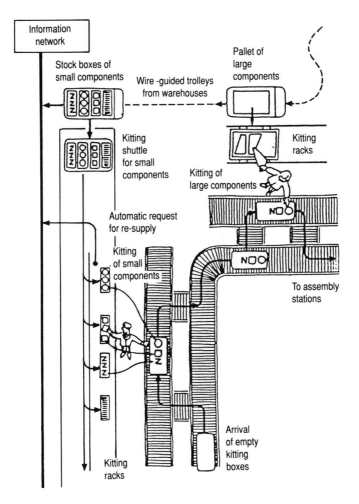

Fig. A.3.4.
'Kitting' and release.

After kitting, the batch consisting of a full kitting box and its tray is automatically routed to the workstation which has generated its release.

A3.4.4   Assembly (Fig. A.3.5)

There are three identical assembly cells in the factory, each containing a kitting set, and 44 workstations. The workstations are independent of each other, thus allowing the operators to vary their timetables.

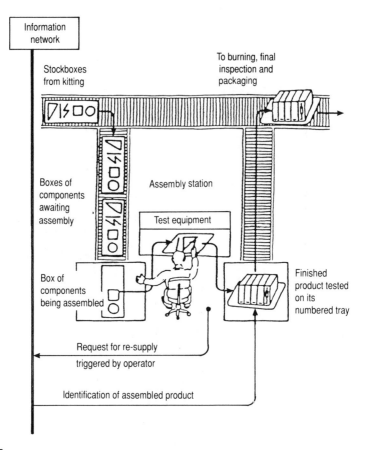

Fig. A.3.5.
Assembly.

The assembly time for the product is about half an hour, with each operator carrying out the complete assembly and testing of the product. Each workstation has in general one product in the process of assembly, one product being tested, one kitting box waiting at the station, and one kitting box en route for the station.

Once the testing has been completed, the product is sent (still on its conveyor tray) by a system of aerial conveyors towards the burning stage.

'Burning' (reliability test) (Fig. A.3.6)

The products arrive in random order. Sorting loops group them into different families for burning.

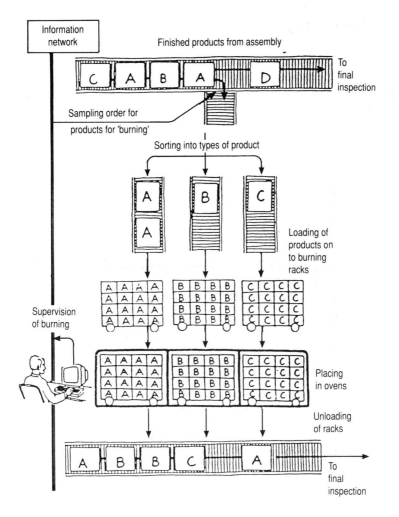

Fig. A.3.6.
'Burning' (reliability check).

When the required number of products belonging to the same family is reached (18 or 36), a rack is full and is automatically loaded into a burning cell. The power supply to the products is then switched on and they undergo dynamic tests with recording of the results. During the tests they are subjected to a high temperature for 24 or 48 hours. They are then discharged on to new sorting loops which feed them through to the final testing stage as requested by that stage.

A3.4.6   Final testing (Fig. A.3.7)

This is to check the effectiveness of the burning tests. If the product passes the test it is sent automatically to the packaging station. Otherwise it is sent to a repair station where the defective components are replaced and is then returned to burning.

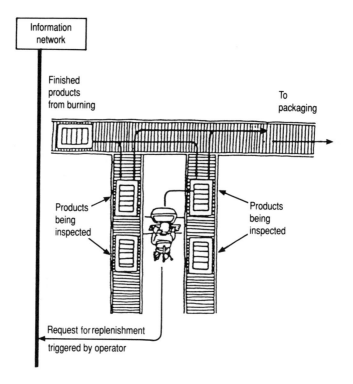

Fig. A.3.7.
Final inspection.

A3.4.7   Packaging (Fig. A.3.8)

These are general-purpose stations, i.e. each can be configured to deal with any type of packaging. The operator has cases, guarantee forms, bundles of connectors and manuals all making up a complete unit for packaging.

A label, carrying text both bar-coded and in ordinary language, and the guarantee form are issued automatically when the product arrives at the

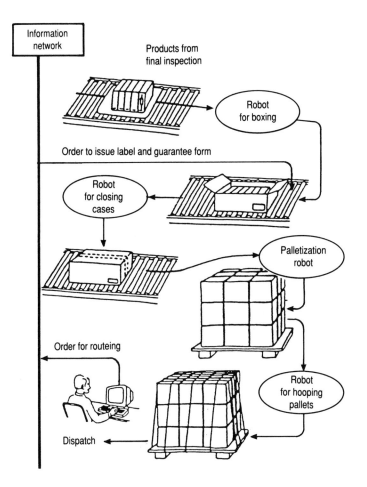

Fig. A.3.8.
Packaging.

station, using information contained in the memory on the conveyor tray. The boxes are routed to machines for final closure and are palletized by a robot. The pallets are automatically hooped and then loaded into trailers ready for dispatch.

Appendix 4
Case Study of Just-in-time Production

A4.1 INTRODUCTION AND CONTEXT

The PSA group, who produce Peugeot, Citroën and Talbot cars, decided to put into practice a set of commercial and logistic principles for producing already ordered vehicles with a very short lead time. The techniques to be adopted were incorporated in a logistic project covering the Citroën and Peugeot ranges, a project defining all the methods for controlling the flow of parts and materials in a quantitative way, starting from their distributors, passing through their factories and means of transport and ending at their suppliers.

The project reflected a need for considerable changes, particularly in production control. The standard method of mixed flow used till then, pushed by forecast demand upstream and pulled by orders from the trade downstream, was abandoned and replaced by a flow system pulled entirely by customers' orders.

Driven by market demand, the diversity in the production of Peugeot cars had become so great that handling a central stock of products was inconceivable. In an annual production of 1.2 million vehicles, there were no less than 30 000 different specifications (the mean annual 'series' of a specification is 40, the most popular model selling only 7000–8000 vehicles per year). It was therefore necessary to operate without a buffer of new cars between production and the retail trade.

Peugeot sells its production to its distributors on a monthly basis, the complete French catalogue containing 15–20 models described by entries such as '405 petrol', '405 diesel', '309 diesel', etc. This 'contract' is smoothed out on a weekly basis. The detailed weekly orders from distributors are known a few hours (three to four) before the physical release of the mechanical components and six working days before the start of assembly.

The industrial diversity inherent in Peugeot cars can be judged from the following statistics. Peugeot has 2000 distributors, 6 car assembly plants (terminal units), 24 other factories and 800 suppliers. Its bills of materials include between 120 000 and 140 000 items for the Peugeot and Citroën ranges and 300 changes per day are made to these. The daily volume of orders for the Peugeot range leads to between 100 000 and 200 000 production orders and between 200 000 and 300 000 handling orders.

A4.2   THE CONSEQUENCES FOR PRODUCTION

Each month and one month in advance, distributors define 20 global quantities (family: 205, 405, etc; fuel: petrol, diesel; etc.; type of body: three-door, etc.). These figures determine less than 15% of the items handled in the bill of materials. The master production schedule thus becomes a highly uncertain tool for 85% of the items and industrial resources.

For those manufacturing processes carried out more than two weeks before the vehicle emerges from the assembly line, control of the production flow is in an uncertain state, even without any technical hitches (Fig. A.4.1). This uncertainty is related to the gap between forecasts and the actual choice of distributors, the effect being particularly noticeable for

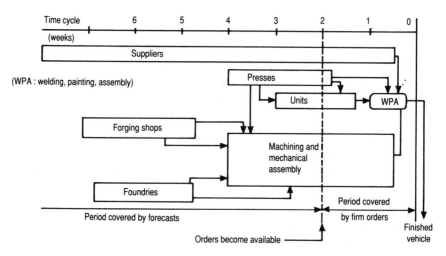

Fig. A.4.1.
The traditional organization of production.

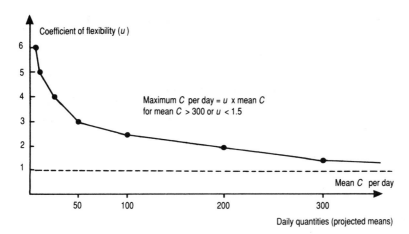

Fig. A.4.2.
Relationship between flexibility and mean daily output of vehicles.

small rates of production (Fig. A.4.2). The gap at a given point may be more than 500%, since it is due both to the variability in market demand and difficulties at the plant.

Thus, to start massive production upstream on the basis of forecasts entails too many errors and uncertainties in the control of the flow of production. With traditional methods, Peugeot can produce only 80–85% of the vehicles ordered each week with the planned standard lead time of 12–13 working days and not the 95% aimed at.

A.4.3   DEVELOPMENT OF THE NEW CONCEPTS

The free daily choice of those involved in the motor trade cannot be accurately forecast (i.e. to within 5%) since it is not in fact a free choice. The only quantitative contracts entered into by the distributors are very general ones: family of car, country, engine power. For the other characteristics of the vehicles, only certain limits can be predicted, i.e. the ranges of variation within which the free choice of distributors will have an impact on an industrial resource. The rule is to have permanently available the maximum daily range of variation in order to meet any possible choice of the trade.

Peugeot defines flexibility as the ability to consume, deliver, and if possible produce, the materials, sub-assemblies, units, . . ., versions and specifications in variable quantities every day, every week, every month, but within predetermined limits.

To meet these objectives, Peugeot considered two different types of method.

(1) *A choice of operations which diversify the products by manufacturing them in a very short time.* This is *delayed diversification,* which logically leads to coordinated flows (coordinated by customer orders).

Coordinated manufacturing orders are a special feature in the field of synchronous control (see sec. 4.5 in Chapter 4), like the assembly of an engine to be installed in a car ordered by the distributor, or a crankcase machined for the same engine. These methods have been known for a long time in the car industry (seats assembled and covered by overlapping operations for a vehicle in process of assembly).

A particularly interesting example is that of the manufacture of shock absorbers for the 605. Since this is a top-of-the-range model, the demands for customization and thus for variety are extremely strong. The vehicle is therefore assembled according to the 'specifications' of the customer, and on this basis the front shock absorber may vary according to a large number of options (fog lights, washers for headlamps, colour of body-work, etc.). This sub-assembly for the finished vehicle must therefore be made very quickly and must then be taken to the car assembly line at the Sochaux Production Centre. The shock absorbers are produced in the plastic components factory at Audincourt at some 10 km from Sochaux. The manufacture of the component is triggered by a synchronous order created by a remote data-communication message generated 219 minutes before the shock absorber is mounted on the vehicle by passing it to a precise point in the production line. The message is received at the Audincourt factory where it initializes a more or less automated production process. The sub-assemblies are then packaged and taken by lorries to Sochaux. There, with no intermediate or temporary storage, they are directed to the assembly station where they are attached to the vehicle in no more than a few minutes.

Flexibility is achieved by the choice of different operations which diversify the products according to manufacturing orders, in a relatively short time (seven working days in September 1992).

(2) *A choice of constituents already diversified and available in sufficient quantities.* These are items in stock or in-process used to provide flexibility, the flow of which is governed by the 'reconstitution of real consumption' principle (RECOR system). This is Kanban, intentionally used to support the variability in demand.

The number of parts in stock depends on the supply and handling times and the maximum daily consumption. A demand equal to or less than this maximum can be satisfied without preparation. The construction of handling and production orders will involve replacing what is consumed after

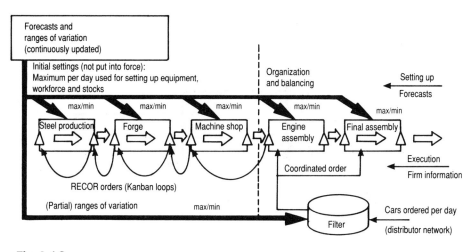

Fig. A.4.3.
The new organization.

physical observation of the consumption. There is thus no calculation of orders and therefore no need to know the contents of the manufacturing orders for the vehicles in order to construct the orders for the foundry and the refinery (i.e. the supply of metals) (see Fig. A.4.3).

Peugeot applies this technique to components whose statistical consumption can be assessed. Consider, for example, shock absorbers for a car lower in the range, the 205. These items are less diversified than those of the 605 and are very suitable for 'reconstitution of consumption' techniques.

In this new organization, the role of the master schedule has changed. It is no longer a closed and fixed form of contract for the operational production, but a tool for preparation which specifies the limits to the variations within which production must be able to comply with the strategic time objectives.

The master production schedule thus plays the role of a framework programme which pre-allocates the resources (equipment, workforce, stocks), making it possible to take on a volume of demand lying between maximum and minimum limits established by forecasts made on the basis of the global quantities supplied by the distributors (Fig. A.4.4).

The new approach makes it essential to become familiar with the form and rhythm of forecasts which no longer consist of firm figures but which involve ranges of variation at all levels of manufacturing and supply. A veritable mutation of the internal culture and of the relationships with subcontractors and suppliers has had to take place.

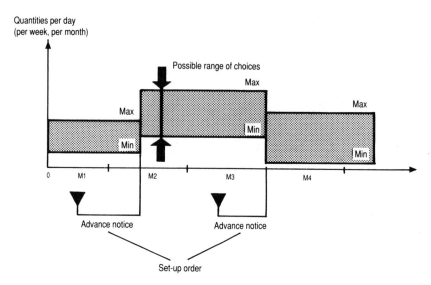

Fig. A.4.4.
Ranges of variations.

The anticipated rewards of this new logistic at Peugeot are promising:

A customer lead time of 30–35 calendar days reduced to 15–20 days.
Considerably increased optimization, and better control, of stocks of components.
Better control over workshop loads and hence a distinctly higher level of production and quality.
Rationalization of the information systems and a better integration of the design, mechanization and production processes.

The project now under way already applies to 40% of the internal production flows at Peugeot. At the moment, less than 15% of the external suppliers' flows of materials are involved. The methods should be in full operation by September 1992.

One great advantage of all this is worth emphasizing: the simplicity of the methods for controlling production flow, their decentralization so that they can be easily understood and their direct application by the skilled workforce, have between them greatly improved the social climate.

Bibliography

AFNOR, *Clés pour un projet de GPAO*, Editions AFNOR, Paris, 1986.

Archier, G. and Serieyx, H. *The Type Three Company*, Nichols Publishing Company, East Brunswick, NJ, 1987.

Ashby, W. Ross, *An Introduction to Cybernetics*, Methuen, London, 1964.

Beer, S. *The Brain of the Firm*, 2nd edition, John Wiley & Sons, Chichester, 1981.

Bounine, J. and Suzaki, K. *Produire juste à temps: les sources de la productivité japonaise*, Masson, Paris, 1986.

Debaecker, H. *Le calcul des structures*, Hermès, Paris, 1988.

Hanson, O. *Design of Computer Data Files*, Pitman, London, 1982.

Henderson, J. M. and Quandt, R. E. *Microeconomic Theory: A Mathematical Approach*, 3rd edition, McGraw-Hill, New York, 1980.

Ingersoll Engineers, *L'usine integrée*, Hermès, Paris, 1988.

Ohmae, K. *Triad Power: The Coming Shape of Global Competition*, Free Press, Macmillan, New York, 1985.

Ohno, T. *Toyota Production System: Beyond Large-scale Production*, Productivity Press, Cambridge, MA, 1988.

Paturel, R. *La comptabilité analytique: système d'information pour le diagnostic et la prise de décision*, Eyrolles, Paris, 1987.

Pujolle, G., Seret, D., Dromard, D. and Horlalt, E. *Integrated Digital Communications Networks*, vol. 2, John Wiley & Sons, New York, 1988.

Sekine, K. *Kanban: gestion de production à zéro stock*, Editions Hommes et Techniques, Paris, 1983.

Shingo, S. *Maîtrise de la production et méthode Kanban*, Editions d'Organisation, Paris, 1984.

Wright, O. *Réussir sa gestion industrielle par la méthode MRP2*, Editions l'Usine Nouvelle, Paris, 1982.

Index

The full expressions for acronyms not defined in this index are given at the first page reference under the appropriate entry.